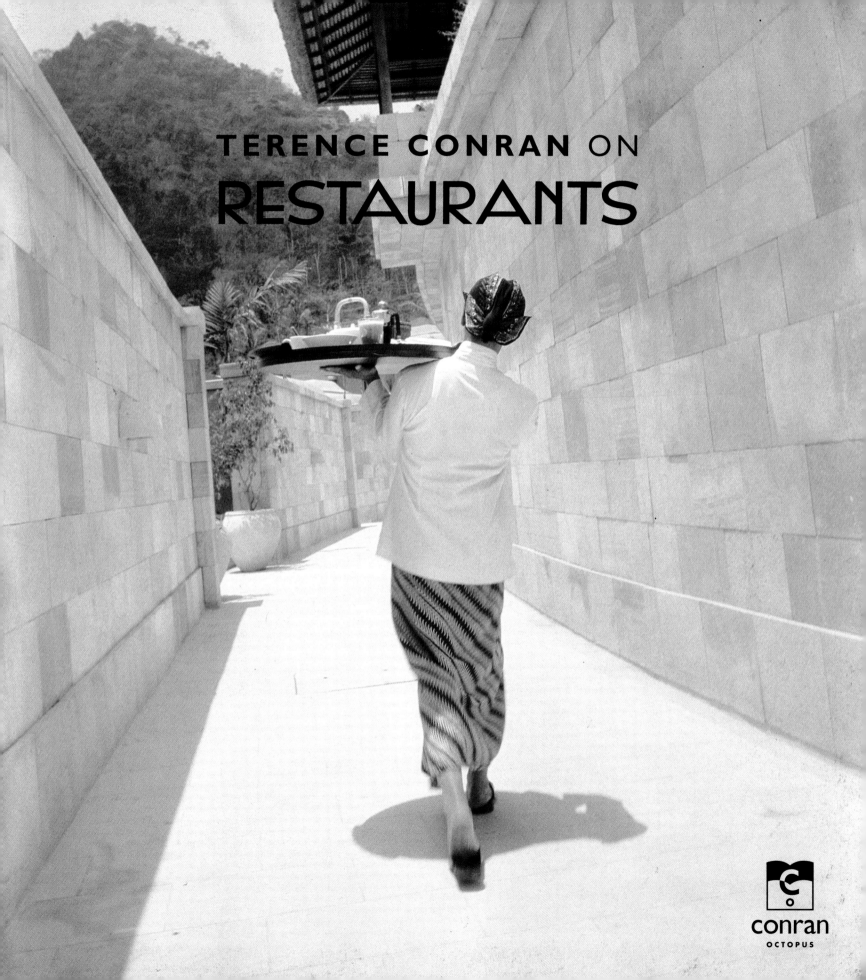

TERENCE CONRAN ON
RESTAURANTS

conran
OCTOPUS

To the cast of characters, both past and present, who have made our restaurants

such a hard act to follow. And to Victoria Davis,

who did most of the hard work.

First published in 2000 by
Conran Octopus Limited
a part of Octopus Publishing Group
2–4 Heron Quays
London E14 4JP

www.conran-octopus.co.uk

ISBN 1 84091 038 0

British Library Cataloguing-in-Publication Data
A catalogue record for this book is available from the British Library
Colour origination by Sang Choi International, Singapore
Printed and bound in Italy

Senior Editor: Emma Clegg
Proofreaders: Colette Campbell and Rosie Hankin
Indexer: Peter Barber

Art Editor and Design: Helen Lewis
Picture Researcher: Nadine Bazar

Production Controller: Sue Bayliss

Project Consultant: Simon Willis
Editorial Advisor: Elizabeth Wilhide

Picture captions:
PAGE 1: kitchen at Orrery, London;
PAGE 2: The Mercer Kitchen, New York;
PAGE 3: waiter at Amankila, Bali; opposite: chef at work;
PAGE 6: Laurel and Hardy in film still from *From Soup to Nuts*, 1928;
PAGE 7: Restaurant De Pastorie, Lichtaart, Belgium.

CONTENTS

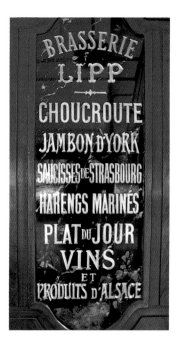

the cockroach
IN THE BLOODSTREAM

I shall never forget my first trip to France: **the abundance of sunshine and colour, wonderful produce and generosity** – everything in total contrast to the unrelenting greyness of post-war Britain. In the early 1950s in London it was difficult to eat out in any style without spending a lot of money. **It seemed obvious that there was an opportunity, so a friend and I decided to open a café.** Neither of us had an iota of restaurant experience but as I had a girlfriend living in Paris, it seemed appropriate that I go and take the plunge. **And so *plongeur* I became, and what an experience!** The kitchen of La Mediterranée was indescribably squalid, a small poky suburb of Cockroach City. My station was at a vast slop sink, and **all I did for the first month was wash pots, pans, dishes, platters, knives, spoons, basins and bowls.** I didn't break much, so was promoted to vegetable boy, which largely consisted of peeling potatoes, the monotony relieved by the odd carrot or artichoke. It was strangely exciting. **A lot of adrenaline flowed, I survived, and I certainly learned a thing or two.**

My first visits to France in the early 1950s were a complete revelation. I was entirely seduced by the fresh produce which was piled high on market stalls, the simplicity of the eating traditions and the integral role that they played in the way the people lived and the relationships that they had with each other. I now maintain that this country taught me not only how to live, it also taught me to eat.

In France I discovered that there always seemed to be time for eating and talking. There were many occasions when we drove through beautiful countryside on open roads, knowing that wherever we stopped there would be somewhere pleasant to linger over a *plat du jour* and a carafe of wine. The food was often quite simple – perhaps nothing more elaborate than a tomato salad, roast chicken, steak and chips or salt cod, accompanied by a local cheese or a fruit tart – but you could guarantee that it would always be delicious and lovingly prepared.

Just the same attitude was evident in the French markets. The exuberance of the traders and their passion for the produce was palpable. And what produce – tables heaped with misshapen tomatoes, radishes and artichokes; baskets of *ratte* potatoes, red peppers and courgettes; scented melons, blushing peaches, firm apricots and little baskets of wild strawberries. Then there were stalls of pungent olives, herbs and spices; rabbits, chickens, hare, quails and pigeons laid out on marble slabs; great trays of cheeses, baskets of butter and pails of crème fraîche; barrels of mussels, clams, fresh tunny fish, squid and monkfish resting on piles of slowly melting ice. The colourful and aromatic spectacle would be swarming with a loud, busy crowd of serious shoppers, each of them intent on selecting the very best produce to eat that day. The rule in France was always that one bought for immediate consumption: I remember being asked by a stall-holder whether the Camembert that I wanted to buy was to be eaten for lunch or dinner!

The sensuality and abundance of those French markets, no less than the *Routier* restaurants with their distinctive red and blue enamelled signs, or the family-run bistros serving plain home-cooked food, made an enormous impression on me: I can still remember a meal of tiny broad beans, baby artichoke hearts and radishes, fresh bread and really good butter, followed by a perfect *omlet fines herbes*, that was eaten in a little beach-side café near St Tropez. I was certainly at an impressionable age, but the lasting impact of those experiences also owed a great deal to the striking contrast that they made to attitudes in Britain at that time.

It is difficult now to imagine the Britain of the immediate post-war years, a time where there was a severe and pinched quality to life. In the early 1950s, the five-shilling price limit placed on restaurant meals, imposed during wartime, had only just been lifted and some types of food were still severely rationed. In London it was extremely difficult to eat out in any style without spending a tremendous amount of money. There were a few grand places to eat – for example hotel dining rooms and restaurants such as the Café de Paris and Boulestin – while at the other end of the scale, there were pie and mash houses, Joe Lyons Corner Houses and caffs, and these bore absolutely no resemblance to the roadside *Routier* restaurants of France. In between these two extremes there was virtually nothing.

Inspired by my trips to France, I recognised immediately the commercial potential of introducing a different type of eating out in Britain. The café that a friend – Ivan Storey – and myself decided to open was based entirely on this instinct. Neither of us had one iota of restaurant experience but my conviction in the idea was strong and this led to my getting a job as a washer-up at La Mediterranée, the Parisian establishment in Place l'Odeon – my experience here, and my promotion to vegetable boy was my true initiation into the business of restaurants.

In the austere years of post-war Britain, food – like much else – was about needs rather than wants. When the influence of other cultures was felt – such as this early pizza parlour – the actual food still owed more to the bland tastes of the British kitchen than to the fresh, flavoursome original.

La Mediterranée in Paris has changed little in its appearance since I worked there as a 'plongeur' in the early 1950s. But in those days, whilst the restaurant the customers saw was really quite grand, the kitchen was an eye-opening thieves' den of squalor and cruelty.

In those days, many chefs were fairly brutal individuals, who were often drunk and abusive, and sometimes dishonest and cruel. After my experiences in the kitchen at La Mediterranée, I wondered whether it would be possible to have a restaurant with no chef at all. A restaurant with no chef? Impossible. But the idea that I came up with was The Soup Kitchen. It was hardly a new idea – the very first use of the term 'restaurant' was applied to an eighteenth-century Parisian shop selling soups and bouillons – but it was original for its time and place.

The Soup Kitchen, which opened in London in 1953, was exceptionally simple in terms of design. Large black and white Fornasetti-style blown-up prints from *Livre de Cuisine* by Jules Gouffé, the nineteenth-century French bible of gastronomy, and a red painted wall made for cheap drama. The black and white floor, tables with metal legs and tiled tops and cane-seated stools (which I designed and made) gave a young, contemporary feel. And there was no chef. Instead we employed a young (mostly female) staff to boil up the cauldron of stock, chop vegetables, ladle out bowls of soup (a shilling for tomato, pea or lentil, 1s 6d for minestrone), cut up baguettes, slice Cheddar cheese and dole out portions of apple tart made by Mrs Trueman in Bethnal Green. We also had the second Gaggia espresso machine in London – that was my favourite job, frothing up the milk for the cappuccinos.

We had sent out flyers to announce the opening of The Soup Kitchen and, at midday on the day in question, we duly expected a horde of bright young things to flock through the doors. Instead, a raggle-taggle band of tramps turned up, evidently expecting a rather different sort of soup kitchen. We hadn't the heart to turn them away and fed them all a bowl of soup (an entire month's profit from the cash-flow projection). Thankfully, the publicity this episode attracted meant that the customers did come in droves after that – the entire cast of *Guys and Dolls*, the hit musical playing at the Coliseum popped in on their opening night and subsequently made it their favourite spot.

Two more Soup Kitchens followed that first venture in Covent Garden and both enjoyed the same success. Then we opened the largest Soup Kitchen of all in Cambridge. It had 150 covers and was always crowded, but at first we could not understand why at the end of the night there would only be about £12 in the till. Then we realized that the students had come in for one espresso or a bowl of soup and stayed talking and debating until closing time. I learned the hard way that turning tables is one of the restaurateur's important skills.

My next foray into the restaurant business came soon after, in 1954, with Orrery. The site was at the 'other end' of the King's Road, opposite The Bluebird Garage. (I can remember sitting in Orrery looking at what was then an ambulance station and thinking how I'd like to get my hands on that space – I only had to wait 40 years.) Orrery occupied the basement and ground floor of a little Georgian building, long since demolished, and there was a walled garden to the rear.

In this period, things were at last beginning to look up in London, as far as eating out was concerned. Amateur avant-garde restaurants were opening, serving new types of food, and there was a palpable air of enthusiasm for cooking in general. Much of the impetus for this change can be traced to the influence of Elizabeth David, whose recently published books, the classics *Mediterranean Food* and *French Provincial Cooking*, brought the sunshine and aromas of French cooking and the experience of France so vividly into our lives. 'Scampi' Bill Stoughton at the Watergate Theatre Club, La Popote and later the Hungry Horse, Hilary James at Le Matelot and La Bicyclette, Walter Baxter, George Perry Smith in Bath, myself, and many others were enormously influenced by her robust and romantic enthusiasm. Nick's Diner, in Ifield Road, a popular bistro owned and run by Nick Clarke, had a menu directly inspired by Elizabeth David. It was also around this time that Egon Ronay, probably the best-known gastronomic name in Britain today, opened a small restaurant, the Marquee, that served *haute cuisine*. *Haute cuisine* had not previously been available outside the grand hotels and large restaurants and, although the restaurant was not very successful financially – Ronay says that he was ten years too early – it was considered by critics to serve the best food in London.

The type of simple French food evocatively described by Elizabeth David, rather than *haute cuisine*, was what I wanted to put on the menu at Orrery – omelettes, grills, bistro food. This time I had a chef, a Pole, who not only worked in the kitchen, but eccentrically slept on top of the ice-cream fridge. My sister Priscilla was a waitress, my parents helped out as washers-up and I did almost everything else. The timing must have been right because Orrery was a success. But we were lucky, too, and a little luck is something every new enterprise needs.

One of the original attractions of the restaurant, from my point of view, was its rear garden. The garden was shaded by three large plane trees; I paved it in York stone slabs and built a barbecue for outdoor grills. The year we opened the weather was unusually fine. Summer began sometime

The truly grand restaurant at the Crillon in Paris is inside. But eating outside in the beautifully proportioned courtyard also has a magical sense of occasion.

around April and seemed to go on well into October. The Orrery's outdoor eating area became very popular with diners seeking to make the most of that rare occurrence, a good English summer.

Orrery was not the first bistro in London. The Harrington Hotel had opened a small basement restaurant in the early 1950s with French waitresses and red-and-white checked tablecloths, and set the scene for the many bistros that came and went over the next few decades. My design for Orrery, however, eschewed this formula in favour of a smartened-up version of The Soup Kitchen design. On the walls and ceiling were large blown-up prints of orreries – I have always been fascinated by these clockwork models of the solar system. The floor was covered in lino and the tables were tiled in black and white.

Like me, many restaurateurs had come into the business from other professions and careers. The Soup Kitchen had been inspired as much by the need to make a bit of money as by my experiences in France – my embryonic furniture business was not yet very profitable. But by the time Orrery had been open about a year, my design and furniture businesses were beginning to take off and, as I needed time to pursue these interests, I sold my share in the restaurant. I was not to return to the restaurant business in a serious fashion for fifteen years or more.

In the years to come, however, my fascination with restaurants, food, markets and cooking simply refused to go away. I wrote and read books and articles about food, designed restaurants for others, ate in the best (and some of the worst) restaurants in the world and constantly talked with friends and colleagues about the pleasures of eating.

By 1971 my growing design business was located in premises in Neal Street, Covent Garden. A vacant ground-floor space under our offices proved just too tempting to ignore and I decided to open another restaurant, partly as a place to entertain clients, partly as a way of demonstrating our company's interior design skills, but chiefly, I suspect, because I simply could not resist the opportunity to get into the restaurant business again. I am particularly proud of The Neal Street Restaurant, which has been owned and run since 1985 by my brother-in-law Antonio Carluccio. In a fickle and often ephemeral trade, it is not often that you find a contemporary interior that has lasted so long and worn so well.

Eating places now began to creep into my other endeavours. When we opened the King's Road Habitat in 1973, in a converted cinema, it included a café. Many subsequent Habitats also made the symbiotic link between eating and shopping by incorporating cafés where shoppers could take a break during the hard work of making purchases. It's accepted nowadays that food adds value to the retail experience – witness the cafés and restaurants within the Joseph and Nicole Farhi shops, for example – but, excluding department stores, I believe we were among the first retailers to make the link as a matter of course.

Acquisition of the Michelin Building in the Fulham Road and its subsequent restoration offered the chance to venture a step further up the gastronomic ladder. Bibendum, opened in 1987, above the relocated Conran Shop, has regularly been rated one of the five best restaurants in London. The Blue Print Café on the first floor of the Design Museum at Butlers Wharf followed in 1989. But from the early 1990s onwards, with the development of the Butlers Wharf Gastrodrome, then Quaglino's and Mezzo, my involvement in restaurants has grown more and more intense.

In the old days, when we were starting out with The Soup Kitchens, most restaurant kitchens were dirty and dingy, homes to cockroaches and worse. Since that time I've always compared the irresistible lure of running a restaurant to having a cockroach in the bloodstream. With a new complex of restaurants and bars opening at the relaunched Great Eastern Hotel in the City of London, the Bridgemarket development in Manhattan nearing completion, and a successful family of London restaurants ranging from Sartoria to Bluebird to Coq d'Argent up and running, I've come to accept that the cockroach is in my bloodstream for good.

The origins of the restaurant

Restaurants as we know them have existed for a relatively short time – which is an astonishing thought when you consider how central food and the pleasures of the table are to life. According to the famous French gastronome Anthelme Brillat-Savarin, it was not until the second half of the eighteenth century that the first restaurants opened; the restaurant's place of origin, unsurprisingly, was Paris.

Up until this time, inns and taverns catered for the needs of travellers, while cafés and coffee houses provided meeting places in towns and cities. For those at the lower end of the social scale with no access to a kitchen or cooking facilities, there were also cook shops, selling precooked food or where a joint of meat could be taken to be roasted or bread to be baked. In France, *traiteurs*, who ran shops that were the precursors of delicatessens, sold ready-made food of rather higher quality and greater sophistication.

In Britain as well as Europe, country inns were usually little better than hostels where the post coaches would stop to feed and water the horses, and where travellers could take a meal or stay the night before continuing their bone-rattling journey. The food on offer was generally pot luck, and the standard of cooking and accommodation variable in the extreme.

Cafés, which had originated in Constantinople in the middle of the sixteenth century, rapidly became popular in Western towns and cities. In such venues one could drink coffee, chocolate – and, later, beer, gin, claret, port and Madeira – read possibly the only newspaper for miles around, gossip, talk politics and literature, play cards and smoke. Predominantly if not exclusively male in clientele, cafés naturally saw the transaction of much business; many companies originated in coffee house associations. The international association of insurance underwriters, Lloyds, started life in 1688 in Edward Lloyd's Coffee House in Lombard Street in the City of London. Anyone wishing to insure a ship or cargo would find there others to 'underwrite the risk' and pay for any loss to the insured goods.

The true concept of a restaurant, however, meaning an establishment with a choice of different dishes and 'specialities' of the house from which customers can choose, dates from the latter part of the eighteenth century. It had its origins in an amusing little dispute that took place in Paris in 1765, when a soup vendor, M Boulanger, applied the term 'restaurant' to describe his soups. Using the word in its original meaning 'that which restores' and with typical commercial hyperbole, the sign over the shop proclaimed 'Boulanger sells restoratives fit for the Gods'. Boulanger, however, was not content to stop at this point; he was ambitious and wished to expand his repertoire. At that time, the culinary guilds were all-powerful; the traiteurs had the monopoly on selling cooked meats in sauces or ragoûts. Boulanger, although he was not a member of the corporation of traiteurs, had the courage to defy this monopoly and offered a new dish to his customers: sheep's feet in white wine sauce. There was an immediate and predictable outcry; the traiteurs brought a lawsuit against Boulanger; but Boulanger finally won the case, which turned on a legal nicety concerning the precise

Café culture swept through Europe in the nineteenth century. People would meet as
often to do business as to socialize, as can perhaps be seen in this coloured woodcut of a
Viennese café (c. 1875) by Ferdinand West.

definition of 'ragoût'. The furore did Boulanger's business no end of good and his dish became wildly popular. Even the king, Louis XV, was curious enough to have it served at Versailles.

Boulanger's establishment was not precisely a restaurant, as we understand it today, but the effect of his entrepreneurial cheek was to loosen the stranglehold of the guilds and to suggest intriguing possibilities to other like-minded individuals. Several other restaurants made an appearance before the Revolution; one, *Aux Trois Frères Provençaux*, opened in 1786 and survived for nearly a century. As *Larousse Gastronomique* records, the restaurant's name provided another early example of creative licence: the three founders of the establishment were neither brothers nor did they hail from Provence.

The French Revolution finally swept away the power of the guilds and corporations, along with the heads of most of the aristocracy. By the beginning of the nineteenth century restaurants had proliferated, providing not only a democratic opportunity to sample the type of cooking that had formerly been enjoyed only by the rich, but also a forum for intellectual life. Many restaurant chefs were the former cooks of recently beheaded aristocrats, while the waiters were newly redundant footmen and valets. This brought *haute cuisine*, previously known only to the rich, within the experience of the general public. These new restaurants were very different from the old inns and taverns whose insalubrious surroundings were legendary, and from the noisy smoky atmosphere of the coffee houses. In their dining salons the customer would be able to sit in grand comfort, usually in his own private dining room, and eat fantastically elaborate and rich food served by waiting staff second to none.

Haute cuisine, surely one of France's greatest exports, spread across Europe and eventually to the New World. One of the key figures in establishing classic French cuisine was the great Marie-Antoine Carême (1784–1833), who had worked his way up the ladder to become the private chef of the French diplomat Prince Talleyrand, Napoleon's most powerful minister. Carême's exposure to the world of diplomacy had convinced him that one of the greatest of diplomatic tools was the provision of memorable and impressive banquets. Trained as a pastry cook, he was renowned for his extraordinary decorative concoctions; he once wrote: 'The fine arts are five in number, to wit: painting, sculpture, poetry, music, architecture – whose main branch is confectionery.' His success was on an heroic scale; he went on to cook for Tsar Alexander, the British Embassy in Paris and Baron de Rothschild as well as the Prince Regent at the Royal Pavilion, Brighton.

Le Grand Véfour is perhaps the most opulent of nineteenth-century Parisian restaurants still remaining. A couple of steps up from the more democratic brasseries such as La Coupole, it's still a buzzing place to go for a special occasion.

The Prince adored Carême's food and complained that he would die from eating too much of it, since it was all so tempting. Carême responded that it was his great concern to stimulate the royal appetite by the variety of his dishes, but that it was no concern of his to curb it. Although Carême stayed in England for only two years, his influence was long-lasting.

The great London hotels and gentlemen's clubs of the nineteenth century were sumptuous establishments. Renowned chefs, such as Alexis Soyer and Auguste Escoffier, who had learned their profession at the stove of the great Carême, helped to establish *haute cuisine* in Britain. Their menus were similarly elaborate.

Alexis Soyer was an important influence on British gastronomy. The *Globe* referred to him in 1841: 'The impression grows on us that the man of this age is neither Sir Robert Peel, nor Lord John Russell nor even Ibrahim Pasha, but Alexis Soyer'. Soyer's excellent pedigree gained him employment at the Reform Club. His first step was immediately to redesign the kitchens, therefore improving their layout and the working conditions. After Soyer's redesign, the Reform's kitchens were considered to be the best and most progressive in Europe.

The Savoy, which promoted the fashion for mixed company dining, employed César Ritz as manager and Escoffier in the kitchen. Lauded for the excellence of his culinary skills, Escoffier became famous, and still is, for his *Guide Culinaire*, published in 1903. It was truly a labour of love, taking 20 years to put together, and containing approximately 5,000 recipes. He was really responsible for pioneering the modern idea of restaurants as we know them today, of eating out, of eating as a pleasure, as an adjunct to travel, and as a leisure activity. The scene was set: with the Prince of Wales, a man known for his gourmandizing, leading the pack, the rich had found an enduring interest in food, wines and eating out.

To César Ritz nothing was too much trouble for the pleasure of his guests. Ludwig Bemelmans' fabulous story, which recounts the tale of Mrs George Washington Kelly's birthday party, complete with flooded ballroom, a replica of her Miami mansion and duplicate birthday cake, was surely inspired by the occasion when Ritz flooded the ground floor of the Savoy to re-create the Grand Canal. Bemelmans' tale illustrates the perspicacity of his fictional maître d'hotel, whose acute sense of 'anticipation' meant that all was not lost when his exacting customer's cake sank to the bottom of the artificial lagoon. The resourceful maître d' had had a duplicate cake made, which he thereupon instantly produced and saved the day.

Such indulgence was for the few. But a taste for good living soon reached the middle classes, and restaurants sprang up all over London. The grand restaurants – Romanov's, the Trocadero, Café Royal – were places of immense luxury. Lavishly decorated, with a wealth of marble and mirror, plush and gilt, potted palms and accompanying orchestra, and huge – the Café Royal could feed more than 650 a night – these restaurants were patronized by the famous and infamous. Still grand but somewhat less glamorous were Simpsons, Rules and Kettners, and their menus reflected this with less elaborate dishes served in more modest surroundings.

In less than a century, restaurants had established themselves as sophisticated venues where those at the upper end of the social scale could indulge in the finest food and wines. In the process they had also influenced the development of cafés and coffee houses, which had been on the scene far longer. In the face of competition from the new restaurants, French cafés became more elegantly decorated in the nineteenth century, attracting the literati, intellectuals and politicians. Aux Deux Magots and Café de Flore in Paris are classic examples of the genre; there is a brass plaque at Deux Magots bearing the name Simone de Beauvoir and marking the place where she habitually sat to write.

An early French variation on the café was the bistro. These evolved as eating places for workers, serving good, plain food, reasonably priced, and so soon attracted impoverished writers, artists and journalists who probably

Ladies who lunch are popularly scorned for having nothing better to do than spend their husbands' money on clothes and expensive meals. Pre-emancipation, ladies lunched – as here, at Delmonico's in New York (1902) – to discuss and address social issues and to raise funds for good causes.

had neither the desire nor the wherewithal to cook. They offered a warm, welcoming atmosphere and became home to many of their clientele. The bistro took hold in towns and villages all over France and some became famous for the excellence of their menus.

One of the largest concentrations of family-run bistros is in Brussels. Perhaps the best known is Mère Jeanne Ducasses, where in a rickety front room, with lacy curtains, no reservations, no menu, no time limit, you can still eat veritable *cuisine de terrior*, simple meals, good seasonal ingredients and loyal creations of classic recipes.

After the bistros came the brasseries, originally attached to the breweries of Alsace and Lorraine, regions which brought their cooking to the big cities along with their beer and coal. Brasseries evolved from inns and their rough and ready wooden tables, foaming tankards of beer and plates of oysters reflected their humble origins. In Paris and other cities they became more elegant, serving refined variations of peasant dishes, often specializing in crustacea and doing a brisk take-away trade in oysters. The brasseries became home to writers, artists and fashionable society, and many were situated near the major railway stations to serve hungry travellers.

In Paris today many of the historic brasseries are still open for business, places like La Coupole, Balzar, Lorraine or Lipp. Opulent or plain, they are always full of interesting people – modish young things, intimate couples, *les anciennes* with their poodles, irascible old gents arguing politics, immaculately

Aux Deux Magots in Paris (1959): when I first went to France and Italy after the war, I was amazed
at how people flocked to cafés and bars, and at how well they could eat for little money.
Our nearest equivalent, the English pub, seemed ridiculously divided according to class and sex.

coiffured *haute bourgeoisie*, and everyone in between, an intoxicating and seductive democratic mix. Brasserie customers can be fiercely loyal. When Balzar was recently acquired by an international firm, a petition was got up by the regulars demanding that not a single thing be changed.

But change is the hallmark of life and the restaurant has undergone great transformations during the twentieth century. The influence of foreign travel has brought exotic flavours and ingredients from all around the globe to the table; much of the formality of the old way of dining out has gone and the distinction between café and bistro, bistro and brasserie, and brasserie and restaurant is no longer clear cut or precisely relevant. This is seen with Tom's in Notting Hill, London, set up by Tom Conran in 1990 and run for five years as a delicatessen. This period saw a dramatic increase in competition from supermarkets and this compromised the shop's market. In response, 50 per cent of the floorspace was devoted to a café, with astounding success.

Despite such adaptations to conventional formats, what does not change is the simple pleasure of eating good food. It may be a brave restaurateur who would put Boulanger's sheep's feet in white wine sauce on his menu today, but food is where it all began and food is what it is all about.

Gastronomic dreams

I have a completely unsubstantiated belief that 92 per cent of the population have at one time or another entertained the notion of owning and running their own café, restaurant, tea shop or pub. And in most cases, I am prepared to bet, those dreams have been inspired by the unique sense of well-being that comes from a really good experience of eating out. Many restaurants around the world have influenced my career as a restaurateur, but I can think of three examples, all of them French, which have been particularly memorable. In each case, it is the food that lingers in the mind, which is ultimately (although not exclusively) how it should be.

Before motorways, if you were travelling south from Paris to Marseilles, it was a two-day journey in all with a stop-over round about Lyon. The area from Dijon to Lyon has been the centre of gastronomy in France for some

We start to eat long before the food arrives on the plate: Brasserie Lipp's neon sign lights up the 6th arrondisement of Paris, luring in the hungry and thirsty; de Boussignac's illustration for boudin sausages gets the mouth salivating.

time: it really is a geographical miracle – with softly rounded hills, an abundance of rivers and the great waterways of the Saône and Rhône running through the centre, bordered by rich alluvial plains. Arguably the best wines in the world are made and bottled in Burgundy. And with great wines, good food follows.

One of the most famous restaurants of the region, and many people's favourite, was La Pyramide, perched on a bluff above the Rhône in the town of Vienne. Here Fernand Point, one of the most important chefs of the early twentieth century, ran his establishment. Point was not a sophisticated man, but he had trained in the grand hotels of the time: the Bristol in Paris, the Imperial in Menton, the Royal in Evian-les-Bains. Once he opened La Pyramide he never had any further desire to leave Vienne. In this restaurant he took the classic *Lyonnais* specialities and made innovations without losing the essential fundamentals of *haute cuisine*. The restaurant became hugely popular under his direction, not only with wealthy English tourists and rich Parisians stopping over *en route* to the south, but with other less well-off but equally enthusiastic travellers.

I could never forget my first visit to La Pyramide. I cannot remember what I had to start, perhaps the *gratin de queues d'ecrivisses* or the *pâté de chasse*, but singularly memorable was what followed, the *poularde de Bresse en vessie*. The dish consisted of a chicken, with slivers of black truffle slipped between the skin and breast, smothered in butter, encased in a pig's bladder and then steamed. When the membrane of the bladder was slit open, the scent of the truffle mingling with the aroma of the chicken juices was incredibly appetizing. It was delicious beyond anything else I have ever tasted. Followed by a local cheese, or *fraises des bois*, a meal here was nothing short of an inspiration.

Nowadays, motorways link the major centres in France but, for the sake of one's sanity, it is essential to leave the autoroute behind and venture on to the N routes. Between Mâcon and Lyons, the old Paris to Marseilles road runs parallel to the A6, west of which lie the gentle rolling hills of Beaujolais. At Romaneche Thorins, best known as the depot of Georges Duboeuf, the wine *negociant*, I recently found a hotel that was well worth the detour. Les Maritonnes is not spectacularly situated; in fact, it is jammed between the

The Routiers sign is a familiar and welcoming site throughout France,
proudly worn by small, family-run restaurants promising good, simple food.

railway and the road, albeit a minor rural road. The welcome, however, is calm and warm. Arriving late one afternoon, hot, dusty and thirsty, we sat under the plane trees, watching a family play *boules* (giving rise to much speculation as to the interfamilial relationships – a favourite pastime) and sipping an excellent *Mâcon Clesse*. It was a good start, and our expectations were reinforced by the smell of a *fonds de veau* cooking and the encouraging sounds of a dinner in preparation coming through the open kitchen window.

The dining room was typical of its kind – French provincial *bourgeoise* – dark wood, lace curtains, potted palms and opalescent glass lamps. The other customers appeared to be extended family groups staying for a week or two – the hotel was evidently considered worthy of a longer sojourn than one night. Tables were impeccably laid and the menu had no pretentions, was not over-ambitious and made intelligent use of local produce. The waitresses were of the school of serious professionalism, courteous yet friendly, who clearly enjoyed our appreciation of the excellent food; a knowledgeable sommelier presided over a comprehensive list. What Les Maritonnes illustrates, I think, is that a slick interior design scheme is not necessary for a successful restaurant. The hotel was comfortable, popular with an apparently loyal clientele and there was simply no need for the dining room to be 'designed'.

Les Maritonnes is situated in an area of good, if not great, food. Not a million miles away – five kilometres to be exact – in the town of Fleurie there is a restaurant of such excellence that I'm actually salivating as I write this. L'Auberge du Cep in the Place Charles de Gaulle serves some of the best food that I've eaten in France. Again, the food is served in a room that is not at all well designed – much too elaborate and fussy for my taste – and which conspicuously fails to reflect the simplicity of its context in the market square of a country village. Madame greets you with steely politesse and heavy menus embossed with gilt are presented. But then it gets really serious. *Cuisses de grenouille a l'ail* – garlicky frogs' legs – *queues de crevette en salade* – prawn salad – all manner of things *truffe* and three varieties of foie gras are just for starters. And for the main courses, *ris et rognon de veau* – veal sweetbreads and kidneys – *volaille fermière au Fleuri, aux morilles*...the only problem when faced with this situation is actually making a choice. On one occasion, my colleagues Joel Kissin, Simon Hopkinson and Bill Baker, making a research trip prior to the launch of Bibendum, found choosing so difficult that they ordered a starter and two main courses each, and followed that with cheese and a pudding!

Such sublime meals are the stuff of dreams. And, if you are like me, it is but a short step from dreaming about great meals you have once enjoyed to the all-consuming desire actually to run a restaurant yourself. There is no doubt that there is something eternally appealing about the idea of a restaurant, perhaps in a country town, with 50 covers, owner-chef in the kitchen, the wife or husband in the front, waiters from the village, vegetables, herbs and eggs from the garden, fish from a nearby river or harbour, organic produce available locally, writing the menu daily according to what is in season... a dream that was so beautifully portrayed in the charming BBC television series *Pie in the Sky*. The reality, however, is often very different, and that is where this book comes in. This is a book about running a restaurant, about being a restaurateur. It is for both armchair dreamers and those with more serious plans to turn their dreams into reality. And it is also for those simply seeking an insight into what goes on behind the scenes.

Running a restaurant is a business like no other. It would be philanthropic bordering on the foolhardy to get into it without intending to make money, but it is certainly not a business for those who are after an easy life. The risks are high, the outcome unpredictable and the integration of diverse disciplines challenging in the extreme. As a business, a restaurant uniquely combines both manufacturing and retail; it is both factory and shop, selling what it makes right on the spot. Creating a restaurant involves the skills of architects, designers and builders, as much as chefs and waiters. Running a restaurant involves finance and management, buying and cost control, at the same time as food preparation, cooking and service. No restaurant will ever succeed unless it is run along sound business lines. But, paradoxically, the very moment customers begin to perceive a restaurant solely as a business enterprise is the moment that restaurant begins to fail.

To open and run a restaurant of moderate size today places a huge range of responsibilities on the shoulders of the would-be restaurateur. There are obvious tasks: pay the rent and local taxes; gas, water, electricity and telephone bills; brief, control and pay various professionals such as architects, designers, engineers, consultants and builders; equip the kitchen; equip and decorate the restaurant; provide the china, glass, cutlery, napkins, tablecloths, towels and soap. Then there is the maintenance: clean the restaurant, kitchen and lavatories; remove the rubbish; wash the china, glass and cutlery; launder the napkins, tablecloths, towels and staff uniforms; repair, replace and redecorate anything that needs it. And so far we've not even served a drink.

Buy the food, wine and spirits; print the menus; take the bookings; cook the food; provide bread and butter, salt and pepper; serve the food and drinks. Make out the bills, collect and bank the money; pay the credit card commission, the VAT, the wages and the tips. Arrange the holidays. Hire and fire the staff. Chase the bad debts and the no-shows, and control the theft...While such tasks may be the ultimate responsibility of the restaurateur, in larger establishments there are managers and other members of staff to share the burden. What is truly miraculous are the small owner-run places where only a few people manage to juggle vastly different roles.

Even today, after a lifetime's experience, on the night I open a new restaurant my hands are quivering. What makes it worthwhile? Chris Bodker of London's Avenue and Circus, who in a former life was an investment banker, says that no other business gives you such instant gratification. To be able to stand in your own restaurant and see enjoyment, pleasure and satisfaction on your customers' faces is the great reward, and it is something you simply do not get making million-dollar investments for clients on the other end of a fax, phone or e-mail.

Being a restaurateur speaks to those instincts that give us, to use a well-worn phrase, the 'feel-good factor'. It's about providing a total experience, the abstract aesthetics of hospitality, comfort, sustenance, conviviality, companionship and entertainment. But, above all, being a restaurateur demands passion.

Restaurants increasingly furnish ways to partake in contemporary culture, and ways in which we can engage with specific places, whether in town or country. In a disjointed world, a restaurant where we feel at home and return to time and again provides an essential sense of shared experience. I hope that this book will inspire you to look at restaurants with both a different perspective and a new appreciation; I also hope it will give some of you the impetus and encouragement to get into the kitchen yourselves. When it does work, it's simply the most wonderful job in the world. Take the plunge!

This photograph by Henri Cartier-Bresson shows a café owner at the start of a new day in Florence: from such basic elements as tables and chairs come the foundations for a city's social life.

location

The café at the Musée d'Orsay in Paris enjoys a magnificent view across the city to the Sacré Coeur.

Finding the right location is the first step to opening a new restaurant. **If you fondly dream of opening your own café or restaurant, it may be that the location goes hand in hand with your dream:** perhaps it is of a smart cocktail bar in a city centre, of a public house in a country backwater or of a seaside café. These associations show the importance that is attached to location: **exceptional views, a building with history or local character can all help create a bit of magic.**

Of course, the received wisdom among property developers is that there are three things to look for in a site: location, location and location. **However, prime sites do not come cheaply,** and the restaurant business is an exceptionally tricky one. Very few restaurants are full from day one, and almost all will go through a painful learning curve during the opening year. The last thing you want is to add to the stress by paying a premium in rent. **For me, it is all about potential.** Analysing the potential of a site and balancing its inherent commercial strengths and weaknesses is the pivotal point on which a restaurant founders or flourishes. **What is required is a balance of careful planning and entrepreneurial vision.**

The threat of bombs spelt an end to the revolving restaurant at the top of the Post Office Tower (as it then was) in London. But there was something magical about the idea of dining in a restaurant that slowly turned as you ate, even though the food was second rate.

It is only once a location is secured that the various other elements of running a restaurant have a context. Everything else follows from it – the type of food, the formality or otherwise of the presentation, the amount spent on fitting out the space. All the time I am turning ideas for restaurants over in my mind and when a site comes up, I can then look at the location and apply one or a combination of these ideas. It is the first stage of finding the site that then kick-starts the whole process. As an energetic restaurant group, Conran restaurants are inundated with rafts of property proposals, most of which are unsuitable – premises may be too big or too small, the lease may be too short or too expensive, but more often than not, the site will be in the wrong place.

Just as finding a good location is one of the most important criteria when you are purchasing a shop or domestic property, it is reasonable to expect the same to hold true when it is a question of acquiring a site for a restaurant; perhaps even more so. After all, launching a restaurant is a major undertaking and one that demands considerable investment. A prime location means customers on the doorstep and a better chance of success.

Or does it? Location is indeed a crucial consideration for the would-be restaurateur, but important distinctions have to be made. When you buy a house, you invariably tie the value of your property into the prosperity, or otherwise, of the immediate neighbourhood. In the urban postcode lottery, everyone is aware that the same type of accommodation can be worth vastly different amounts depending on the area. The success of a restaurant, however, is not exclusively a function of its site. In many cases, restaurants can act as spurs for regeneration, breathing new life into what were formerly rather moribund areas.

In this particular context, it is crucial to distinguish between 'destination' restaurants and those dependent on passing trade. The concept of the destination restaurant is enshrined in the famous phrase from the Michelin Guide: *vaut le détour* or 'worth the detour'. It's part of the formula of the destination restaurant to be off pitch, a little removed from the beaten track. A restaurant that relies on passing trade for most of its custom, on the other hand, has to be sited right in the heart of things. This is why fast food outlets and hamburger chains go to such lengths to acquire sites in busy shopping streets, and why you never need to use a routefinder to locate them.

Economics

The optimum location for a restaurant is one where there is a guaranteed catchment of customers both during the day and at night: for example, where there is some office business but also a good residential area for evening bookings. Such sites are hard to find. The economics of running a restaurant today are such that the figures only work if you have lunch as well as evening trade. Seven good lunches and seven excellent dinners is a restaurateur's dream but that usually only happens when there is the right balance between office and residential property in the immediate neighbourhood. A good lunch trade and a reasonable dinner is acceptable; even preferable is to have a good lunch and an excellent dinner business at least six days a week. It's hard, although not impossible, to make a success of anything less. Our Paris restaurant, Alcazar, suffers somewhat from being situated in an area in which there are few offices. Alcazar does excellent business in the evenings, but lunches can be slow. Another case in point is our Zinc Bar & Grill, situated in Heddon Street, a back street off Regent's Street. Heddon Street is also

Sitting outside in the dappled sunlight in early summer, it's difficult to imagine a more perfect place for a restaurant than the Colombe d'Or in St Paul de Vence.

SHAUN HILL
Chef and owner of
The Merchant House,
Ludlow, Shropshire

Over the past 30 years, the restaurants that I've been working in have been getting smaller and smaller. These days, I wake up, look in the shaving mirror and know immediately that my kitchen is fully staffed. The restaurant premises are also my home. I do all the shopping, cooking and washing up. My wife Anja works the front-of-house with one other person and they both help me in the kitchen.

The lifestyle seems idyllic, but it does mean you have to work long hours. There are so many jobs to do. The joy is that the parameters are set by you and not by a bank. When I left the country house hotel Gidleigh Park in Devon, I received several offers to front up the kind of restaurants where you pretend it's your place but it's actually owned by men in suits. I didn't want to do that. Chefs generally don't amass any real capital so the only way for me to have my own place was to do it on a small scale.

Working small isn't necessarily a narrowing of ambitions. Not reporting to a board of directors means I can take the decisions that don't make business sense – for example, I can choose to spend too much on food. I have no pressure to recoup the outlay within three years, no pressures other than the target I set myself, which is to offer a level of cooking excellence over and above what a place like this would normally be expected to provide.

Food is number one for me: people come here for the grub, and to enjoy my idea of what good grub is. In the mornings, I go round the shops like a 1950s' housewife, looking at ingredients and poking them before I buy. I type the menus myself every night at six o'clock, so right up until then the dishes can be whatever I want. There are things we can't do on this scale, such as lavish pastries, but I can give attention to the aspects of cooking that are normally neglected by head chefs, such as the vegetables.

There is profit to be made from working on a small scale but not a lot. I do this because it's what I want to do. I only need to pull in 20 people a night. If I had to pull in 200 I'd be thinking differently. We have another room that we could put tables in and we could open more days of the week than we do, but the ratio of preparation time to service has to be carefully controlled. I calculated seven services was the maximum I could cope with without taking on another kitchen person. If I had more staff, I would become a hostage to fluctuations in the trade. It makes no difference to me if, on a wintry Wednesday, only six people turn up, but it would make a difference if I had more staff.

I don't claim my way is right, it is just a reflection of my priorities. My former reputation as chef at Gidleigh Park has helped a little, but cooks working on a craft scale will always attract people locally if they are any good – they might just take a little longer to become established. If you have no name, it's best to open up next door to someone who has, so that you can be compared favourably. We came to Ludlow because we wanted to be somewhere that was nice and had cheap property. The risk was minimal because in turn the outlay was minimal. Now Ludlow is chock-a-block with restaurants – three have a Michelin star – and yet they have all opened in the time since we came here.

home to a successful Moroccan restaurant, Momo, a good example of a 'destination' restaurant drawing customers into this relative backwater in the evening. Zinc, however, was intended to function more as a corner café, and has to work much harder to attract passing trade.

Given these economic parameters, it is more and more difficult to make a success of that persistent dream, the country restaurant. Even in rural France, where many excellent restaurants operate, very often on a family-run basis, times are getting harder. In the country, invariably everyone wants to eat out on Friday and Saturday night, sometimes at Sunday lunchtime. The result is that the dining room is empty four or five nights a week and over-subscribed the rest of the time. I know of a really superb restaurant outside Lyons that had to close last year after being in business for some twenty years. It just could not afford the overheads on what had become effectively a two-day week.

Country restaurants can work, however, as shown by the conspicuous success of The Merchant House, Shaun Hill's restaurant in Ludlow, which boasts a Michelin star. And when they do work, they can have a beneficial role in the revitalization of the whole area. Ludlow, a small market town that was once the capital of the Welsh Marches, has population of only 10,000. Over the last decade it has become renowned for the excellence of its food and now holds an annual food festival. As well as Shaun Hill's restaurant, there are two others with Michelin stars, six butchers, two delicatessens, and a high-quality greengrocer and fruiterer – as well as numerous other places to eat and stay. The excellence of the restaurants attracts tourists to the area, and in turn creates a demand and a ready market to sustain quality suppliers – all in all, a country version of a gastrodrome.

Perhaps the easiest way for a budget-conscious entrepreneur to become a restaurateur is to take over an existing restaurant. It is essential to carry out plenty of research beforehand to establish exactly how the restaurant operates, what its customer base is like, how good a relationship it has with other local traders, and what changes you might make for the better. Be prepared to pay more for a successful business with a high goodwill value. If you are considering taking over an under-performing business, you must find out why it is not successful and how feasible it will be to overcome the problems. Avoid those locations that have seen a succession of enterprises fail. There are some sites that look good on paper

Quaglino's in St James's, London, is in a basement – not, on the face of it, an ideal location. But the name
resonated with fond memories of the 1930s, when the original Quaglino's was the toast of London society.
A bold entrance, dramatically lit at night, provides a hint of what lies beyond.

and ought to work, but for some mysterious reason never do – the Chinese might ascribe the run of bad luck to poor *fong chui*, but opening a restaurant is chancy enough without taking on such additional risk.

Des Gunewardena is chief executive of the Conran restaurants and handles their finances and property deals. We are increasingly known for making successful restaurants in what others might perceive to be 'difficult' locations. Des believes that there are many advantages in not going into prime locations – lower property costs, for one thing, little if any competition, and the opportunity to negotiate a favourable lease or rental terms.

All our restaurants are located slightly off the beaten track – Quaglino's is just off Jermyn Street; Mezzo may be in Soho but it is a block away from the heart of things. Even Bluebird, although it is situated on the King's Road, is at what has always been considered to be the quiet and unfashionable end. Butlers Wharf, which was possibly the most difficult location to develop, has turned out to be very successful despite the fact that access is far from easy, with city lunchers having to travel across the river and evening diners coming from distant locations.

The first step when the site comes up is to make an assessment of the viability of the location. Is there enough local business to fill a restaurant at lunchtime and sufficient interest to attract diners in the evening? How much space is there? How much will be front- and how much back-of-house?

How many covers? What turnover and what profit is the site likely to generate? The demographics of the area will also give you an indication of the type of customers you are likely to attract – business people in the financial districts, ladies who lunch in an upmarket shopping area, literati in a publishing quarter, media moguls where you find ad agencies and luvvies in theatreland. This catchment, in turn, will give you an idea of the sort of food to serve and the prices to charge. Before he bought the site that became the restaurant Bank, Tony Alan stood in the street and counted how many people walked past: the day's total of 10,000 indicated a pretty good chance of passing trade.

Many restaurants have failed even before they got off the ground quite simply because of under-investment. It is crucially important to get this right from the beginning: under-capitalization at the start makes catching up, once the restaurant is open, very, very difficult. Start with a basic business plan that will show you if your proposal has economic feasibility. You should know what sort of restaurant it will be, who your likely customers are, and therefore the kind of menu, the price range and the style of interior design. It is particularly important to ensure that enough money is put into the restaurant behind the scenes. This is where people often try to take shortcuts, but the right equipment and the right standards of efficiency and hygiene are essential.

Alcazar, in Paris, was originally a printing works then a popular cabaret-bar, famous for its transvestite performers. When we were approached with the idea of reviving its former glories, Alcazar was empty and falling apart; but the process of rebuilding it revealed both the potential of the space and reminders of its past.

It is invaluable at this stage in the process to bring in an architect or designer to give you an idea of the cost of the project and also an accountant who has some knowledge and experience of the business. These people will be able to advise you on how much operating capital you are realistically likely to need for the type of restaurant that you are planning. There are given formulae that can be applied for assessing the viability of opening a restaurant – food pricing, margins and resulting profit. Satisfying the often conflicting demands of regulatory bodies and local authority departments means that you will probably need more capital than you think. On the other hand, borrowing too much capital up front can be just as foolhardy as under-investment in the project, bearing in mind penalties such as the high rates of interest that a new and risky enterprise usually has to pay. Getting it right means taking sound financial advice and doing your homework well.

The property deal can make a huge difference to the ultimate success of the restaurant. The basic rules are: do not spend too much on rent and tie the rent wherever possible to turnover. Conran restaurants do not acquire a site to make a rapid return on the investment. Instead, we look at the long term and try to negotiate long leases. Because the company spends a great deal of money on design and fitting out a restaurant to high specifications, the property deal must be sufficiently good for the business to be viable not only in good times but also in bad. It does not take a crystal ball to predict that over 15 or 20 years there are going to be highs and lows in the business; therefore the object should be to keep the fixed costs as low as possible. One way to achieve this is to negotiate a relatively low basic rental with the landlord, with the balance tied into a percentage of the turnover. This is the way we try to do business and the strategy then protects the company should there be a fall-off in the restaurant trade some time in the future.

One of the best property deals that we have so far negotiated was for the site of The Conran Shop and the Orrery restaurant in Marylebone High Street. We were able to secure a 99-year lease on very beneficial terms on the understanding that the shop and restaurant would significantly regenerate the area, which in turn would be of benefit to the landlord who owns substantial amounts of property in the same vicinity. Indeed, the case has now been proved with local rents rising by an average of 70 per cent since we arrived.

Restaurants are increasingly seen as attractive opportunities for investment. Chris Bodker, proprietor of Avenue and Circus, relies on large groups of investors to finance his restaurants. I believe that if investors are faced with a management team that has commercial integrity and a good track record, something different to offer and sound business sense, the investment potential should automatically speak for itself. But, as an investment opportunity, a restaurant also provides something a little more special than a unit trust or a multinational corporation, and that is the opportunity to actually participate in the development of the enterprise. People always love the idea of going to a restaurant and thinking: 'I own part of this.' Shared ownership can be a very real part of the restaurant's 'feel-good factor'.

Rules and regulations

Many restaurateurs almost come to the point of suicide before they even open their doors in their desperate attempts to unravel the nightmarish tangle of official regulations. It is important to be well prepared for this assault on your nerves; it is one aspect of opening and running a restaurant that simply cannot be approached in a naive spirit of hopeful optimism. It is therefore essential for anybody who is planning their own restaurant to find out about the regulations that apply *before* they begin the project. They should also be aware that such regulations tend to escalate in number and complexity every year. In my experience, the truly frustrating aspect of the whole process is that different departments do not coordinate their requirements, work to the same rulebook or even appear to communicate with each other. You may satisfy the demands of environmental health, for example, only to discover that what you are planning will contravene fire regulations. It is often the case that neither side will budge and neither will talk to each other, which leaves you hanging in the middle trying to find a compromise that will be to the satisfaction of both parties. This situation is altogether something of a bureaucratic hydra and at times can drive even the most inspired restaurateur to despair.

The first set of regulations you are likely to encounter are those regarding zoning. These vary from place to place, city to city and country to country. In Britain, local authorites determine the type of business you can operate within a particular zone. Zones designated A1 are for general retailing. In such zones, you can open a restaurant or food outlet only as long as you do not cook on the premises and do not serve alcohol. Such restrictions account for the proliferation of sandwich shops like Prêt à Manger, soup and juice bars, coffee shops and patisseries. Zoning can affect the availability and consequently the price of space – there is a great deal more property on the market zoned for retail use than property designated A3, which allows you to cook and serve alcohol.

But this is only the start of it. Part of the process of assessing the viability of a particular location is to work out how easy or difficult it is going to be to meet the official regulations. If a particular site requires a great deal of work to comply with the rules, the costs may start to soar out of control, however right the location may be otherwise. Is there disabled access? What are the arrangements for getting rubbish out for collection and storing it between times? Are there neighbours who will object to kitchen noise? Is the location accessible for deliveries of fresh meat, vegetables, wine and spirits at all times, day and night? What provision can be made for kitchen extract? If you plan to have air conditioning, where will the plant go? One cannot simply assume, either, that all local authorities will share the same points of view. In some London boroughs, for example, it is virtually impossible to gain permission to install a wood-fired oven; other councils are perfectly relaxed about it.

Gaining permission for A3 use is extremely complicated. You have to take into account health and safety, environmental health and licensing legislation, not to mention fire regulations. All are a minefield of potential transgressions, transgressions that can close a restaurant or prevent it ever opening. Before a restaurant can open it must undergo inspections by all the relevant bodies; all these inspections must be signed off before you can apply to the magistrates for an alcohol licence, and without a licence it is fairly difficult to open your restaurant. Unfortunately, it is not unknown for the environmental health officer to come along and specify exits in one particular place, only to be followed by the fire officer who wants exits in a completely different location. And not until they are both satisfied will you finally get that all-important licence to serve alcohol.

In Europe, EC regulations add a new layer of complexity. A recent stipulation is that 'dirty' plates cannot pass plates filled with food; in other words, you cannot load different shelves in a service lift with plates cleared from tables and plates coming from the kitchen. There now must be separate lifts; moreover, these lifts cannot be next to each other, but must be at least six metres apart. From the same source comes the rule that boxes of fresh food – fruit, for example – cannot be carried through a kitchen area where food, even the same food, is being prepared. Meat, fish, fruit and vegetables must also be prepared in separate, isolated areas, enclosed by walls and with their own entrance doors. The resulting maze of passages makes for an incredibly complicated use of space, which is difficult to plan and expensive to build and operate.

DAS SREEDHARAN
Owner, Rasa Restaurants

❝ My first restaurant specializing in vegetarian food from the Kerala region of India was in Stoke Newington, north-east London. I had been managing another restaurant nearby for a while and knew a lot of local people. Another attraction of the area was that Stoke Newington seems to have the highest population of vegetarians of anywhere in London and they are tremendously loyal customers. I saved up and, with the financial support of a friend, took over the site of a failed restaurant. My wife and I decorated it simply but colourfully – not only because we were on a limited budget and did not want to borrow from a bank, but because we felt the most important thing was to focus on the food and service. At that time, people tended to expect vegetarian restaurants to be run more like coffee shops anyway.

The restaurant turned out to be a huge success. People were prepared to spend a great deal of money enjoying good vegetarian food. We noticed, too, that many people were travelling all the way across London to eat at Rasa and, after a good review in the *Zagat's* guide, we welcomed many customers from America. The idea began to formulate that we should open another branch, more central, more upmarket. Several people had come to us with proposals and we decided to set up a company with one other major investor – an English businessman who had been a loyal customer and became a friend.

When launching Rasa W1 we again took over the site of a failed restaurant, but this one was in shabby condition. We spent £500,000 redecorating and renovating the building to be a much classier restaurant than the former. The food prices were a little more expensive, too, but after some favourable reviews and publicity, the restaurant really took off.

Soon after, we were offered the premises of Interlude, a lovely but struggling restaurant on Charlotte Street, not terribly far away from Rasa W1. It seemed the ideal opportunity to open a place specializing in the seafood dishes of Kerala, a cuisine not previously available in London, and a good means of reaching the people who normally shy away from visiting a vegetarian restaurant. The decoration and equipment at Interlude were already to a very high standard and we felt no need to change it significantly. We simply replaced the *objets d'art* with some Indian artefacts and managed to spend only £10,000 on the interior.

Although all our kitchens are in the basements of the premises, generally considered unfavourable from a logistic point of view, I find the cost of outfitting a kitchen for our style of cooking comparatively inexpensive. We often buy good second-hand equipment from restaurants that are closing down, so the main kitchen outlay for us tends to be on installing the right air conditioning and extractors. Much more expensive are the fancy interior design elements, such as marble floors and good lighting.

The fact that a site may have been a failing restaurant is not a deterrant to me. I have always enjoyed taking something that is struggling and making it a success. We offer very unusual, very high-quality food and have a particularly fine standard of service, which make our restaurants a destination for food lovers regardless of any previously perceived problems with the location. We plan to open a few more restaurants in London, then take on New York, a city we believe is really hungry for this type of cooking. ❞

One of our more complex developments was Mezzo. When we first saw the site – the former Marquee Club – in 1993, it was an indescribably squalid black hole. It took a great deal of imagination to see past the dereliction to the potential of this historic location. The site was hugely complicated, not least because a developer was converting the upper floors into loft-style apartments, the services for which would have to be channelled through our property on the ground floor and basement levels. The basement did not have enough headroom and the floor had to be dug out. An incredibly complicated ducted air management system, together with goods-in/rubbish-out arrangements, electricity, plumbing, sound insulation and IT servicing had to be accommodated – and all this before we could even begin to work on a design concept.

Such complexities, however, almost pale into insignificance beside the tortuous bureaucracy I encountered in Paris when I opened Alcazar, my first restaurant outside London. We had to seek and gain something like 29 separate permissions.

It was a very hot day in late July when I first saw the site. We had been looking for a Parisian location for both a Conran Shop and a restaurant for quite some time – we had found a great deal of proportior available, but none viable from a cost point of view. I was familiar with the area, St Germain de Près, with its art galleries and publishers, and fond of the lively food market on Rue de Buci.

The entrance to Alcazar was very unprepossessing – graffiti-daubed doors, a narrow passageway – but then I saw the magic of the place. Though shabby, the basic space was magnificent: a glass skylight running the length of the room, a wonderful courtyard, elegant columns and a gallery, together with the whole drama of a narrow street entrance giving on to a much larger space. I could see the restaurant filled with flowers, people, bustling waiters, sun, colour, warmth. I also knew that there would be an awful lot to do before that vision became a reality.

The fabric of the building, which originally had been a printing works, was in a terrible state – rickety, structurally unsound, held together with plasterboard and flimsy stud walls. The skylight let in not only sunshine but rain, and obviously had to be replaced. This itself posed an enormous problem. In France any structural addition to a building has to be awarded a certificate called a PV by the fire department. To gain the PV it must be demonstrated that the structure can withstand fire for 60 minutes. How do you prove this? You build a structure and, in controlled conditions, you set fire to it. Simple yes, but wildly expensive. The only possible alternative was to commission the replacement roof from one of the two manufacturers who produce fully certified roofs. Unfortunately, to avoid any chance of not being awarded the PV, these manufacturers adopt a sort of belt-and-braces approach and strenuously over-specify the materials, so that the replacement roof turned out to be hugely clunky. Other than pay for the entire structure to be built twice – one to set fire to, one to install – there was no option but to live with it.

And this is just one element of many. Thirteen different departments – with responsibilities for the roof, sanitation, fire, signage, and so on – had to be informed, pleaded with and cajoled into approving the plans before we could submit them for a *permit de demolir* and then a *permit de construire*. Once the plans were lodged with the planning department, there was then a minimum wait of four months before we could even expect to get the stamp of approval. We were working to a much tighter schedule than that timetable would allow, so we just had to take the risk and start building.

Having seen many, many kitchens in existing restaurants in Paris, the stringency of these laws is obviously new, and most certainly not retrospective. I believe such legislation is preventing the refurbishment and renovation badly needed in a large number of Parisian bistros, cafés and brasseries, and may be stifling the entrepreneurial desire of people who would otherwise jump at the chance to open a restaurant or get involved in such an enterprise. This has led me to believe that Alcazar is the only truly legal restaurant in France!

While some of the nannyish regulations regarding food hygiene often strike me as misguided, they are no doubt inspired in part by some of the well-publicized food scares of recent years. Restaurant refrigeration levels, for example, are extremely tightly controlled and regularly monitored; the same cannot be said of the fridges in most people's kitchens at home. In addition, domestic kitchens are subject to hardly any fire or safety controls, despite them being the most common environment for household accidents. Restaurant kitchens, as one might expect, are required by law to follow extremely stringent safety procedures and standards. And with over two million customers every year, and over 2,000 staff, it is essential to ensure that the Conran restaurants have the best equipment, and that staff are fully trained, to minimise any risk of accidents. Remember that all the investment of money, time and aggravation which goes into meeting these regulations is ultimately worth it.

Worth the detour

Occasionally details of a property land on my desk which give me a *frisson* of excitement. Market research is all very well, but I have learned to trust that gut feeling. If I had merely listened to the experts when planning the Gastrodrome at Butlers Wharf, it would never have happened. There was universal agreement that no-one would be prepared to cross the river for lunch, and the very idea that people would do so for dinner was considered laughable. But stroll along the river walk on a summer evening today and see the people filling the restaurants, spilling outside on to the terraces... My instinct had told me that the pleasure of being able to sit in a restaurant on the banks of the Thames with that incredible view of Tower Bridge before you would outweigh any perceived inconvenience in getting there.

Being prepared to take the risk of opening a restaurant off the beaten track or in a hitherto overlooked spot can lead you to sites that contribute positively to the whole experience of eating out. The City of London, for example, might seem an unusual place to open a restaurant. Although the City in centuries past marked the entire extent of London, the City today is a very strange phenomenon, bustling with people and traffic during the day, quiet as a tomb at night. When we first considered opening the restaurant that would become Coq d'Argent, however, there were increasing signs of life within the Square Mile after six o'clock in the evening. Following the deregulation of the financial markets, traders often have to be at their desks when the Far Eastern exchanges open or stay until the Dow Jones closes. The revitalization of the Barbican Theatre has brought another source of custom to the City, as has the growth of Clerkenwell and Spitalfields as residential areas. It was with a certain confidence that we took on the space at the top of Number One Poultry.

Historically and architecturally the location is unsurpassed. On the site of the former Mappin and Webb silversmiths, facing the Mansion House and flanking the Bank of England, Number One Poultry is the British architect James Stirling's last building, a modern landmark that the current Prince of Wales once compared to a 1930s' wireless set. The restaurant, on the seventh floor of the building and surrounded by a lush roof garden, derives its name from the location. *Coq* refers to 'Poultry'; *Argent* is a play on 'Sterling', the Mappin and Webb building and its location above Bank underground station. When I told Peter Palumbo, co-owner of the site, what we had decided to call it, he immediately replied: 'But why not Les Poules Dorées?' I said I hoped a few golden chickens would come home to roost there.

The message that there is now somewhere glamorous to eat in the City will gradually trickle into people's minds. Coq d'Argent needed some marketing at first, but the restaurant occupies such a special site that we believe that people will also find it worth the trip at weekends.

The Michelin Building, too, is a landmark edifice, with its marvellous faïence façade and soaring stained-glass windows portraying the portly figure of M. Bibendum. When Paul Hamlyn and I bought the building from the Michelin company in 1986, and embarked on an ambitious programme to restore it, the principal intention was to provide space for publishing offices and a Conran Shop. But at the same time it seemed the perfect opportunity to open a restaurant, even though at that time nearly 15 years ago Brompton Cross, the location of the Michelin Building, was not very much of a destination for either retail or food. Paul and I share a passionate interest in both food and restaurants. I also had the hunch that Simon Hopkinson could well prove to be the best chef in London. The result was Bibendum, which has gone from strength to strength. The light in that first-floor space has a magical quality, changing from hour to hour, day to day, season to season. It gives the room a calmness that immediately inspires a feeling of relaxation and enjoyment. And Brompton Cross, which superficially seemed out of the way years ago, now has other thriving shops and places to eat.

Rather similar to the Michelin Building is our Bridgemarket development in New York, Guastavino's. This amazing location, which has not been properly used since the war, is a mere four blocks from Bloomingdales and a stone's throw from the wealthy enclave of Sutton Place. It is right under the noses of the inhabitants of the richest zip code in the world – literally, as it is sited under the 59th Street bridge. Bridgemarket was designed and built in 1909 by the Spanish-born engineer Raphael Guastavino, who designed the Oyster Bar in Grand Central Station. The 40-foot-high main space, with its handkerchief arches lined with herringbone tiling, is listed and the structure itself cannot be tampered with. Bridgemarket was originally a farmer's market where fresh produce was sold in the heart of Manhattan; before the war, the market closed and the site was used as a storage space for road signs. About 15 years ago, there was an idea to revive the food market, but vociferous opposition from local residents called a halt to the plans. I have been interested in Bridgemarket for five years and it has taken a great deal of hard work to bring my vision of a food market/restaurant/retail emporium to fruition. But despite the fact that the site has been overlooked and neglected for so long, I have great faith in the location. From a planning point of view, there are a lot of things going for it. As it is essentially an island site, organizing deliveries and rubbish collection is easier. The rental is low considering the affluence of the surrounding area, and there are no neighbours to complain about restaurant noise – the only disturbance is the trucks that rumble over the bridge.

Another site that has been sitting under everyone's noses for a long time is the Great Eastern Hotel, which is sited right next to Liverpool Street Station. This Victorian station hotel is actually the only hotel in the City – which in itself is a bizarre thought – and was ripe for regeneration. Far from being a location off the beaten track, the area positively swarms with passing trade, commuters using the station, office workers and business people in search of a decent lunch or somewhere to have a drink after work. The Conran group has been responsible for the development of the various restaurants that are located on the site, a cluster of eateries ranging from Aurora, a smart restaurant whose listed interior features a stained-glass dome and Pre-Raphaelite-style frescoes, to Miyabi, a Japanese food bar. There's also Terminus, a bar and grill; Fish Market, a champagne and oyster bar; George, a wood-panelled pub; as well as a private club, banqueting and party rooms. All the restaurants can be accessed from either hotel or street. The idea has been to turn the Great Eastern into a destination which offers a variety of choices, rather than a monolithic statement. The mix both reflects and serves its location.

The flip side of a restaurant expressing sensitivity to site and location is the theme restaurant or chain. I think it is the apparent refusal of the chain restaurant to acknowledge its surroundings that is ultimately so depressing. By imposing a prepackaged identity on a location regardless of where it might be, the chain restaurant essentially thumbs its nose at its own neighbourhood.

Having said that, I do believe that there is an excellent example of how a chain of restaurants can be optimistic, forward-thinking and enduringly popular. Pizza Express was founded by Peter Boizot, a man who was noted for his passions, not only for food but also for jazz and hockey. Boizot's basic idea was very simple – a combination of real pizza, pleasing surroundings, excellent staff, consistent quality and an uncomplicated menu, with the additional bonus of first-class jazz played in some of the venues. Rather than becoming a heartless chain, Pizza Express has evolved into a necklace, as Peter Boizot would say, of really good, neighbourhood restaurants offering inexpensive, good quality food, entertainment and great value for money.

As a basic theme, pizza has plenty to recommend it. The raw materials are cheap and of consistent quality, always available and easily cooked by someone who needs very little training. The end result usually looks and smells good and is sufficiently filling: indeed a fine and honest example of what fast food should be.

The first Pizza Express opened in 1959. Unable to find a satisfactory pizza in London, Boizot was determined to open his own pizzeria. After a long search he found a failing restaurant in Wardour Street. The restaurant was bought for £100 from the widow of the former owner and came with a £14,000 liability and an introduction to Enzo Apicella who was to go on to design many a Pizza Express, as well as other restaurants, in the cool, functional style that was his hallmark. This was pioneering work – at that time the British expected chips with everything and selling slices of pizza was slow to take off. High rents in the West End and pizza at a giveaway price was not a recipe for success and Boizot sought the counsel of a financial brain who recommended moving a bit upmarket: the pizza, hitherto served on a sheet of greaseproof paper, was to be served on china plates, albeit sourced from Woolworths.

But perseverance eventually paid off and within two years another branch opened, this one featuring the first of Enzo Appicella's interiors. The rest, as they say, is history. Today, some 30 years later, the company, with over 170 restaurants, has a turnover in excess of £1 billion and is considered to be the leading purveyor of upmarket pizzas. But the success of Pizza Express does not begin and end with pizzas, with or without the china plates. Pizza Express has managed that very difficult balance of conveying a strong identity in each one of its locations, while respecting and enhancing the unique spatial qualities that each site has to offer. One of the early, smaller branches in Museum Street in Bloomsbury is in a converted dairy. The original tiling is a striking feature of the interior, and is an architectural element that many other chains would have attempted to obliterate. A more recent example is the Oxford Pizza Express. During the course of building work, a sixteenth-century painted wall was uncovered. In response to this discovery, the archaeologists were brought in, the wall was thoroughly documented and has now been sensitively preserved and incorporated into the design of the Pizza Express interior.

Pizza Express at Deanhaugh Street in Edinburgh shows how an historic location can be adapted for modern use. Although listed buildings frequently carry extra restrictions about what can be done, these are often compensated for by the location and the unique character of the site.

TriBeCa Grill, New York

A restaurant's location in a city can dramatically affect its business: if the area is dense with office workers, lunchtimes may be full, but evenings could prove difficult. Sometimes, restaurants can act as a landmark or anchor, as with the TriBeCa Grill which was fundamental to the colonization of that part of downtown Manhattan. Setting up a restaurant in the shadows of a landmark historic building helps to guarantee a steady stream of customers, whilst the spectacular views from the Oxo Building situated on the Thames have helped to make it one of London's most memorable restaurants.

Street café in Rome, outside the Pantheon

Coast, London

Wagamama, London

Amsterdam, Amsterdam

The Oxo Tower Restaurant, Oxo Building, London

Nepenthe Restaurant, Big Sur, California

Whitstable Oyster Company, Kent

Llansantffraed Court Hotel, Abergavenny

Countryside restaurants operate at a more sedate pace. Most customers will have travelled to the area, often specifically to visit a particular restaurant. In warm climates, the opportunity to provide outdoor seating capitalizes on nature's glories; in less certain climes, simple rooms indoors can still benefit from the local views. Space, simplicity, and menus that reflect local produce and seasons seem to me to capture the essence of what makes country restaurants so enduring.

Café in Crete

In Manhattan recently, I went to a restaurant described to me as 'über-chic': so fashionable that it didn't need to advertise its presence from the street. Few businesses can afford the luxury of such an attitude, and certainly not once the first wave of fashionability has passed. Entrances and signs should give a clue, I think, of the type of restaurant that lies beyond the front door, whether it's the welcoming charm of a Spanish local café, the open-armed embrace of a casual Orient-themed restaurant or the slightly old-fashioned values of one of Paris's oldest restaurants.

Restaurant entrance in Andalucia

L'Escargot, Paris

Big Bowl, Chicago

Noho Restaurant, London

Social, London

*You'll have **no scandal while you dine,**
But honest talk and wholesome wine.*

ALFRED, LORD TENNYSON

Landmark, Los Angeles International Airport

New York Grill at Park Hyatt, Tokyo

Jockey Club, Hong Kong

Jules Verne, Eiffel Tower, Paris

La Maison Blanche, Paris

Mondrian, Los Angeles

Restaurants with a view can't help making you feel a little bit special: some restaurants are about theatre and role-playing, whether they are temples of gastronomy or themed chains. Cosseted in a smart, exclusive restaurant whilst looking out at the crowds or the sprawling city, customers feel that they have finally arrived.

Chichicastenango, Guatemala

Ayo's Restaurant, Nerja

Fish market, Istanbul

Senso Unico, Brisbane

Fruit from a Mexican market stall

On the hoof or in a hurry, eating out doesn't always mean sitting down for three courses and coffee. And casual dinners can be memorably special, particularly when we find ourselves transported to a different country and culture: for many people, grabbing a hot-dog or drinking coffee in the Empire Diner is as much a quintessential 'New York experience' as the Staten Island Ferry or a trip up the World Trade Center. Equally, food markets throw us into the smells and flavours and foods of a new place, and are frequently far more 'authentic' than the tourist versions of local dishes that get served in comfortable hotels. Such street restaurants are often temporary set-ups, and flout many of the supposed rules about what makes a successful restaurant: they depend on spur of the moment and passing trade: imagine trying to recommend to someone the particular stall at which you ate the best-ever lamb tagine in Marrakech's night market (OVERLEAF).

Hot-dog stand, New York

Reunification train at Dang Ha Station

Street café, Brussels

Empire Diner, New York

Jellies from La Paz, Bolivia

If an earthquake were to engulf England tomorrow, **the English would manage to meet and dine** *somewhere ... just to celebrate the event.*

BLANCHARD JERROLD

(OVERLEAF) Night market, Marrakech

Beach restaurant, Dieppe

Restaurant in Mallorca

Sydney Harbour, the canals of Venice, the Thames, the Seine . . .
the attraction of waterside locations is impossible to
overestimate. By the river or by the sea, there's a romantic
air attached to such locations that is difficult to beat.

Restaurant in Lisbon

Gastrodrome, London

Da Raffaele, Venice

The River Café, New York

space

The Lenbach restaurant in Munich imports a bold, modern aesthetic to the wedding-cake-baroque interior of the listed nineteenth-century interior of the Bernheimer Palace.

Restaurant design is one of the most complex and challenging briefs that you can give an architect or interior designer. You may have a clear idea of how the restaurant should look, but before any detailed planning of the fittings and fixtures it is necessary to address the complicated logistics of accommodating the various utilities and supplies. Quite frankly, **it is many of the things you don't (or shouldn't) see that are the most expensive to deal with:** proper ventilation, heating and cooling; goods in and waste out; health, safety and fire regulations; and all those things that are taken for granted, such as lighting, water, gas and electricity.

It is only once this infrastructure is in place that you can begin to have fun with your ideas for the front-of-house fit-out. Decisions need to be made about how you will divide the space, where you might put the bar, whether there will be changes of level, what the different views will be like. **Even then, of course, it is essential at the same time to consider how the space will be used from a practical perspective** when it's filled not only with customers, but also with cooks in the kitchen and waiters in the restaurant.

All aspects of creating a restaurant are interrelated. The potential of a particular space may influence the choice of location; in turn, the location may suggest a design approach. Both a restaurant's location and the fundamental qualities of the space itself may also have a bearing on the menu. None of these decisions can be taken entirely in isolation. In a good restaurant, everything comes together to provide a total experience.

Some people seem to view restaurants that are well designed with an element of suspicion. The implication of such distrust is that design is a gloss which conceals deficiencies in the cooking, or that it represents a cynical attempt to sell a restaurant on looks alone. Michelin inspectors have long demonstrated a blind spot when it comes to design; many starred French restaurants, where the food is as superb as you would expect, have frankly atrocious decor. I would argue that good food tastes even better in beautiful surroundings: if the cooking is of the highest standard, why should the restaurant interior not reflect this quality? This is not to say that every restaurant should be lavishly fitted out or provide a showcase for cutting-edge design, simply that the aesthetics of where you eat can be just as important as what you eat, and can go a long way towards promoting a sense of anticipation, enjoyment and conviviality.

A couple of years ago I was in Sydney, one of the best places in the world to find modern cooking. Along with Melbourne and Perth, the city has supplied many a London restaurant with chefs of great talent, whose innovative, fresh and exciting culinary ideas have added immeasurably to the revitalization of the London restaurant scene. I was taken by a journalist on a tour of the new restaurants, cafés and wine-bars in the centre of town and in areas such as Paddington and Double Bay. Bill's was particularly lovely: light, airy, relaxed. The focus of the interior was a large communal table, in the centre of which stood a bowl of nobbly lemons with their leaves still attached. At the time of our visit, four o'clock in the afternoon, a variety of people were sitting round the table leisurely reading journals and magazines and having afternoon tea. The menu featured different combinations of flavours, quirky but not absurdly so, and the whole atmosphere was uplifting and immensely hospitable. Nothing about Bill's was showy; the tremendous sense of well-being that the place managed to convey had been achieved very economically and with the simplest of means.

Another of my favourite restaurants is also in Sydney, Bennelong in the Sydney Opera House, now sadly no longer under the direction of the incomparable and legendary Gay Bilson. The setting and location have to be among the most fortunate in the world – few twentieth-century buildings are so memorable or indeed so instantly identifiable. The restaurant, sited in the smallest of the three distinct super-structures, is modern in the very best sense of the word and in no way compromises the purity of the building's form. Huge tables, dressed only in white cloths, provide theatrical impact when you arrive; plates, glasses, cutlery and lamps are only added piece by piece after you are seated. Then there is the robustness of the menu. The food is superb – deft, delicious and original. The interior is all the more interesting because the design team had to work within the constraints of this architectural landmark: windows for walls, and a ceiling so far away it cannot properly be considered a ceiling at all. The entire restaurant was a masterful blend of style and substance.

What both these examples illustrate, I think, is that good design can enhance both location and ambience and go some way to providing that mysterious X-factor that makes a restaurant truly memorable. But spatial design, from the restaurateur's point of view, must also be hard-working. Getting the basics right – the disposition of space, the architectural shell, the servicing and so on – makes all the difference between a restaurant that is efficient and practical to run and one that loses money and goodwill hand over fist from the day it opens.

Claridge's bar in London has been sensitively redesigned by David Collins to reflect its Edwardian heritage but to update the qualities of a gentlemen's club to the present day.

Back to front

When I start to design a restaurant, I realize that it is just about the most challenging and indeed most interesting design job there is. As I have mentioned before, in simple terms a restaurant is a factory and a shop, and the design must answer all those demands made by both manufacture and retailing. Add in graphics, ergonomics, servicing and technology – together with the need to provide the intangible qualities of atmosphere and welcome – and you have a design brief that covers nearly every discipline.

I find that the easiest way to get a sensitive feel for the spaces and the constraints of a location is to build a simple model of the premises in white card. The actual physical presence of a model provides a real sense of the three-dimensional qualities of a space, unlike a sketch plan, an architectural drawing or even a 3D computer schematic. It is at this stage that I start to see how to arrange the layout.

Often a first-time restaurateur will plan a space starting with the tables and chairs and work from there, from front-of-house to back-of-house, as it were. This is a mistake. One of the worst disadvantages a restaurant can have is too small a kitchen, with service and storage areas that are unable to cope with the number of covers needed to generate a profit. Instead, it is more useful to plan all the behind-the-scenes requirements first – air management, refrigeration, storage, utilities, goods in, rubbish out, staff lockers, administration, IT, cloakrooms, lavatories and so on – and put the tables and chairs in the space that is left. Of course, this is something of a simplistic statement – it would be foolish to install kitchens, prep areas, storage and refrigeration to service 100 covers only to be left with room for 50 – but it is nevertheless worth working to a rough front- to back-of-house ratio of 50:50. This is the ratio to which we try to work but invariably the back-of-house gets the lion's share, with its allocation being anything between 55 and 60 per cent of the available space.

At the same time, flexibility is important, and the type of restaurant you are going to run and the building you inherit will have an effect on the disposition of the space. A pizzeria, for example, demands less back-of-house space because most of the preparation and cooking can be done within the restaurant area itself. Similarly, the kitchen at Zinc Bar & Grill, which has a large prep area in the basement, is quite small. Smaller kitchens are also generally found in restaurants at the luxury end of the market, which demand more space between tables, more waiter stations and serving areas than a casual brasserie or bistro.

When I sat down to plan Mezzo, I realized that the space was far too big to accommodate just one restaurant, and the idea arose to have two levels of dining – one smart, on the basement level, called Mezzo, the other more casual at street level, called Mezzonine, the two linked by a staircase and united by a vast double-storey wall of glass screening the two kitchens. The narrow street entrance immediately gave on to this large space, which was just crying out for the addition of a long, curving bar on the Mezzonine level. Two more areas that had direct access to Wardour Street became the bakery and café.

Bluebird, our gastrodrome on the King's Road, was planned to incorporate a restaurant, café, dining club, food store and chef shop. We allocated space to each of these operations based on our experience and our assessment of the area, its residents and the likely passing trade. The restaurant performed very well from the start, which is what we had hoped and planned for. However, it became clear very quickly that the café was far more popular than we had anticipated – there were queues round the block on sunny summer weekends – while the food store and chef shop were not generating the required turnover for the areas they occupied. It took time, and many headaches, but we rationalized the spaces, enlarged the café, and rejigged the layout of the food market. The result is a far tighter, more efficient and profitable operation. Because the new layout is easier to

Bluebird makes bold use of a converted garage on the King's Road. The
floor of the restaurant is a slab that hangs from the steel roof girders, and
the design plays up this feat of engineering.

manage, staff are happier and the needs of customers are better met. Even with experience, it's possible to get things wrong, which is why you should build in as much flexibility as you can to accommodate future changes.

In the early stages of planning the space, it is important to consult designers, architects and surveyors to work out how much needs to be spent on refurbishment, structural alteration or fit-out. If the project is not large and complicated, a builder who has experience in restaurant or retail fit-out can be an economic option. It can also be useful to consult other restaurateurs to find out how much they spent on their own businesses. A crude guideline is to allow between £1,000 and £2,000 per square metre. This rule of thumb provides, of course, a large margin of differential – costs will tend to be at the higher end of the scale in a city rather than in a rural location. It's also essential to bear in mind that building costs never go down and almost always escalate, especially when you are converting an existing building. Allow a generous amount for contingency and try to avoid making last-minute changes to your plans, which are always hugely expensive.

Planning the kitchen

The chef's job starts well before the restaurant opens. When you have found a location and decided on the type of restaurant you wish to open, it is important to have input from the chef and management at the early stage of the design. A restaurant kitchen is an environment where a team of people produce a great variety and quantity of dishes working under considerable pressure and in conditions which can be fairly extreme. To create the most efficient working space you will need to know how the chef prefers to work and the equipment he will require in order to produce the dishes on the menu. How much prep area is required? How much storage space? Is space needed for a grill, deep frying or rotisserie? Will you need quantities of ice (you will if you serve crustacea)? In Zinc Bar & Grill, for instance, a large area needed to be devoted to a grill, well-serviced by air extraction, to enable the chefs to cook within the restaurant. Cold storage, ambient storage, wash-up areas and freezers also need careful planning in order to establish the most efficient layout.

The design of a restaurant kitchen is highly complex. We employ a specialist in kitchen engineering and contract out the technical work to a catering design practice which works with our own specialists to interpret the brief. In servicing terms, the single most important element is air management. Heat, smoke, steam and the smell of cooking must be efficiently extracted, with the extract outlet raised above the roofline of the adjoining buildings. In turn, cool air must be brought in to ensure conditions in the kitchen remain workable. When we first opened Mezzo there were, as there always are, teething troubles, one of which was that the fish refrigerator broke down. The rapidly deteriorating fish was bagged in refuse sacks and put into the service bay behind the restaurant to be picked up by the local council. Unfortunately, it was an unseasonally warm day, the council truck got held up and the bags had been placed just below the fresh-air intake. The chefs and managers were perplexed by the increasing smell of rotting fish – they had, after all, completely cleared out the broken-down refrigerator and yet the smell was getting stronger and stronger. It didn't take them long to track down the cause.

Overlaying the requirements of the chef and his staff are statutory health regulations, which specify everything from colour-coded chopping boards and knives for different types of produce, to completely separate areas for each stage of production. To prevent cross-contamination and provide ideal, hygienic conditions, many fittings and types of equipment have to be duplicated or triplicated: separate refrigerators for storing raw ingredients before preparation, and chilling the finished product afterwards; one temperature zone for meat and vegetables, another for fish and dairy, and yet another for wines, beers and waters; different sinks for fish preparation, vegetable preparation, hand washing, pot washing and kitchen cleaning. And the tiles have to be grouted with anti-bacterial mastic. These legal requirements have added immeasurably to the basic start-up costs of opening a restaurant in recent years.

Equal attention must be paid to the logistics of deliveries, goods in and waste out, as is given to the cooking and refrigeration equipment. Walkways that are non-slip and easy to clean are essential and they must also be wide enough to take a trolley of raw ingredients or allow access for maintenance of equipment. Staff have to have somewhere to change, shower, store their personal items, eat and rest, and chefs have to have somewhere to telephone, fax or e-mail their suppliers. Durable surfaces and good lighting are also essential. But before a single oven is installed or one tap plumbed in, the foundations of the services – electrics, gas, IT, water and drainage – have to be in place.

Large restaurant kitchens are increasingly dependent on sophisticated technology and an area has to be allocated and designed for electronic systems for ordering, billing, cost and stock control, deliveries and

warehousing. The resulting miles of cables that connect waiters with chefs, chefs with buyers and delivery men, and control security cameras and alarms have to be planned and installed at the time of construction. In this context, the great advantage of a small restaurant is that it can survive perfectly well with only the low-tech assistance of a reservations book, shouted orders and hand-written bills!

There is a tendency nowadays to over-equip restaurant kitchens. Not only is this expensive but it leads to excruciating maintenance costs. The one area where high specification definitely pays off, however, is the piano – the chef's colloquial term for the cooking range – which has to survive a punishing existence. Installing a comparatively inexpensive stove is false economy; we use Rorgue, a famous French foundry, who custom-build stoves to our specifications. A good piano is built like a tank to withstand the warfare of the kitchen. Nevertheless, one of our 'tanks' was destroyed by cleaners who persistently dowsed it with buckets of cold water every night in a misguided attempt to cool it down.

Integrating services and equipment efficiently in the space available demands exceptionally precise planning. Having equipment custom-designed and built adds an extra layer of difficulty to the equation. When the piano was installed in the kitchen at Quaglino's it was a perfect fit – when it was cold, that is. When it was fired for the first time, the heat expanded the stove by an additional five centimetres and knocked down the side wall.

Restaurant kitchens today are a far cry from the poky hell-holes of days gone by, sizzling infernos of heat and bad tempers. High standards of equipping and fitting out have not merely been the inevitable result of official regulations, but have also arisen through the gradual realization on the part of restaurateurs that good working conditions mean happier staff and hence better food at the end of the day. Along with improvements in basic kitchen conditions has also come greater visibility. In the old days, food emerged from behind the kitchen door as if by magic and customers were largely ignorant of what went on behind the scenes. Today, the barriers are coming down: for customers, seeing a kitchen in full swing, the balletic choreography of movement as orders are processed, sharpens the sense of anticipation and provides an element of theatre. For the chefs, catching sight of customers enjoying themselves brings a new level of satisfaction to their work and helps to break down the traditional hostility between front-of-house and back-of-house staff.

Kitchen visibility is far from new. Traditional Mediterranean tavernas and grills are often places where the food is prepared and cooked in full view; and even where kitchens are separate it is common for customers to be invited backstage to choose the ingredients of their meals and approve the level of care taken over their preparation. In the East, particularly Japan, the showmanship of cooks is legendary.

There's a lovely old restaurant in Paris, Chez Alard, where the kitchen is straight in front of you as you enter. The sight and sound of the chefs cooking, plating or exchanging a bit of banter serves as an excellent aperitif. On a much grander scale is the sublime kitchen of Troisgros in Roanne. Having outgrown their existing kitchen, the Troisgros family decided to build a new one from scratch. It incorporates some really intelligent elements – the hot air generated from the ovens is directed to a heat exchanger and

Andrée Putman's design for this sushi restaurant in a Parisian hotel orientates the restaurant around the 'conveyor (kai ten) sushi'. Sympathetic lighting makes the space appear more intimate and sophisticated than many other sushi restaurants based on the kai ten principle.

powers the air cooling. But it is the aesthetic of this kitchen that is so special – it features a polished steel ceiling, beautiful copper pans and a lively little dining area for the head chefs to meet customers and suppliers. The enormous pride Michel and his father have in their kitchen has made all the investment worthwhile.

I first began to experiment with kitchen visibility at Le Pont de la Tour in Butlers Wharf. Large portholes in the double doors of the kitchen enable customers to catch a glimpse of activity behind the scenes. The bar/grill where the chef works at a black slate counter is also visible through a large window. Outside, at the back of the restaurant, an expanse of glazing provides passers-by with a full view of the kitchen and serves as a 'shop window' advertising the hard work required to achieve the delights available inside.

Our first fully open kitchen was at Quaglino's, but Mezzo, with its kitchens arranged on two levels, fully visible behind a glazed wall, takes the strategy further still. The advantages of such assessibility are considerable. Kitchens on view have to be able to withstand scrutiny, and this means having more sympathetic conditions for the staff and better morale.

For customers, one of the more positive outcomes is that it makes the experience of eating out more natural and less contrived.

Comfort levels

Designing a restaurant is not merely a rigorous technical and practical exercise, it also means paying attention to seemingly intangible elements that can make all the difference to the enjoyment of your customers. Sound levels, proximity of other diners and sympathetic lighting are key factors in creating a good ambience.

The sense of well-being which is so important in creating a successful restaurant is also a function of its style. Very few of us, maybe with the exception of minimalist architects, prefer to dine in monastic surroundings; while plain refectory tables, unrelenting hard surfaces and bare walls may be right for a quick lunch, such surroundings do not succeed in giving people incentives to linger any more than they encourage relaxation. At the same time, the type of enveloping luxury that was typical of the grand hotel dining rooms of the past can be just too suffocatingly baroque for today's customers, who are increasingly ill at ease both with excessive formality and with over-the-top soft furnishings.

The preference at the Conran restaurants towards transforming derelict sites grants us some freedom when it comes to design, but restaurateurs often face the challenge of updating existing venues. Oustau de Baumanière is a sympathetic and gentle modernization that has been implemented to dramatic and positive effect. Set in an old olive mill beneath a ruined castle in Provence, it was first opened in the mid-1940s, after restoration work had been carried out despite the constraints of wartime. Owner Raymond Thuillier was an insurance salesman, aged 50, who had decided virtually overnight to become a restaurateur and hotelier.

Archive photographs reveal the hotel's original interior as having an austere simplicity. Thuillier's reputation as a chef grew rapidly and he was awarded three Michelin stars within ten years. With fame and fortune came a corresponding increase in the level of decoration: a swag here, a tassel there, heavy velvet drapes and baroque furniture. This same trend was apparent throughout France, and indeed Britain, during the post-war years presumably in reaction to the restrictions imposed by the war.

At Troisgros in Roanne, the family Troisgros manage a beautiful, modern kitchen with steely attention to detail. The restaurant's three Michelin stars are jealously guarded.

The hotel became a well-known watering hole among the rich and famous, with a guest book that read like *Who's Who*. H. M. Queen Elizabeth II stayed at Baumanière – her first and, for some time, only experience of staying in an hotel. In 1970 Thuillier's grandson Jean André succeeded his grandfather in the kitchen and was recognized as heir apparent. Jean André could see that the hotel's decoration was no longer in keeping with the expectations of their customers. His grandfather, not unreasonably, was afraid that too much change would alienate his loyal clients, so a phased plan of renovation was adopted and carried out over a protracted period. Michelle Halard, a French interior designer of great sensitivity, was called upon to make the transformation, and the final result is pared-down simplicity in line with today's tastes but which does not sacrifice the vital element of comfort.

From time to time our designers have been called upon to come up with a scheme for a listed interior. One such commission was for Lenbach, a restaurant in Munich whose nineteenth-century architectural detailing might well have been lifted straight from a wedding cake. Our solution was to come up with a design that did not take a back seat to the elaborate plasterwork and gilt, but provided a strong contemporary counterpoint. A backlit blue floor unites the space and serves as a graphic contrast to the ornate ceiling. Even more of a challenge has been Bern's, in Stockholm, originally a concert hall and more recently a music hall and restaurant. Bern's is a very romantic space, like a small nineteenth-century gilded opera house, full of history and chandeliers. Our job has been to clean and repair the fabulous shell of the building and make the space work as a contemporary restaurant, bar, grill and café without disturbing the glamorous rococo interior. Light sources have been hidden and all modern introductions kept as simple and elegant as possible to provide comfort and efficiency without arguing with the flamboyance of the architecture.

The architecture of a space can provide drama and theatre, but seemingly less momentous elements also have an important part to play in creating atmosphere. Outdoor eating, for example, is synonymous with pleasure for many people. At Butlers Wharf, where we have three restaurants with tables on the river walk and one with tables on a terrace, nothing short of a blizzard will deter diners from eating outside. We have canopies to keep off the rain and ingenious heaters for chilly days, which provide the necessary physical comfort for people to sit outdoors from Easter to Hallowe'en. Our unpredictable English weather, however, can cause problems. A day that starts grey and with little promise can, by 11 o'clock, have turned into a

An underlit glass walkway makes a dramatic entrance to Lenbach restaurant in Munich. The mix of old and new respects the building's heritage, but makes no apologies for introducing materials and designs that look to the future.

LEIGH PRENTICE

Leigh Prentice and Associates
Architects, Sydney

❝ It is easy to treat restaurant design as a frivolous exercise when really, given the huge amounts of money, effort and reputation involved, it should be approached with caution. Of far greater importance to the eventual success of a restaurant are the location, service, food, prices and the delivery of a consistent product, but it is a pity to squander the opportunity to employ truly contemporary architecture in this potent mix.

Although the restaurants and cafés I design are often described as 'minimalist', a lot of restaurant reviewers use the term generally to describe any contemporary dining room that is even slightly pared back. In fact, there are degrees of any style, and there will always be successful and unsuccessful examples. Minimalism has become a pejorative term and consequently restaurants whose design includes superfluous detail are now considered good simply because they avoid the minimalist 'trap' – as if to suggest the so-called minimalist designer has been lazy or, worse, fashionable. In the process, restaurant reviewers have somewhat tainted the role good contemporary architecture can and should play in creating a restaurant.

A cosy atmosphere can certainly be achieved in a minimalist restaurant, providing the space is not positively barren. To avoid an unforgiving atmosphere, all elements should be carefully coordinated and exploited. The table setting is a focus for the diner, and it can be used, along with a good-looking menu, an upholstered chair, intimate lighting, uniforms and so on, to offset an otherwise rigorous design. The success of a room ultimately depends on the diner feeling a sense of wellbeing. Whatever the style, this comes down to the usual architectural principles: balance, proportion, harmony and massing.

I believe that the design process should be a reductive one in which early decisions are constantly reviewed and discarded as necessary in the light of the developing brief or site. White card working models are a very reliable tool in the design process, as both the architect and the restaurateur can appreciate the space best with a physical model. Computer modelling can be useful to test every aspect of a solution, once you have the basic layout and space resolved, as it allows you to see the space from every possible angle. However, sample or finishes boards tend to be dangerous presentation aids. Although the architect's palette may look delightful in miniature, when translated to full scale the result can sometimes be overwrought.

In most cases, the work of designing a restaurant is ongoing, as the restaurateur modifies the service or responds to the demands of the market place. I've been commissioned to revisit one of my designs on a couple of occasions and I'm very grateful when a client does contact me in those situations. Often restaurateurs don't appreciate the impact that a seemingly innocuous alteration can have on a room. Restaurants are not like private houses in that respect; private spaces can accommodate much more of the personality of the occupant. ❞

blistering scorcher; the challenge for the kitchen and waiting staff is then to cater for nearly double the expected covers. And an unexpected thunderstorm can have everyone outside suddenly wanting to sit inside, creating similar havoc for the management and other diners who have to put up with the temporary commotion.

One of the most important aspects to consider when planning a restaurant interior is the quality of light: how it will be achieved, how it will change from day to night, whether there will be natural light, street lighting and other external influences. Yuji Tsuboi of U Design in Tokyo reiterates the importance of this element of space. 'Lighting is a crucial factor, because it leaves the greatest impression on the customer and contributes significantly to the overall mood.'

Back in the 1950s, at the time when I had designed Walter Baxter's restaurant on the Old Brompton Road, I was given a lesson in restaurant lighting by Vivien Leigh, star of *Gone with the Wind*. I had installed what I thought to be rather glamourous downlighting: Miss Leigh begged to differ, believing the lighting revealed imperfections in her incomparable face, and informed me that ladies preferred soft rosy lighting when dining in the evening. I painted the insides of the shades pink the next day. What this story illustrates, I believe, aside from the insecurities that beset famous stars, is how much lighting contributes to our sense of comfort and ease.

Natural light conditions may include bright, sunny midsummer evenings, overcast midwinter lunchtimes and every variation in between. Even if the restaurant has no natural light source, it is important for artificial lighting to echo conditions outside: people are acutely sensitive and responsive to light and immediately feel uneasy in an obviously artificial atmosphere.

The design of Quaglino's imposed certain difficulties in this respect: the restaurant is situated at basement level and receives no natural light at all. I first saw the site in 1991, when I was in the midst of negotiations for what would subsequently be the location of Le Pont de la Tour. Joel Kissin, then managing director of the restaurant group, had urged me to take a look at

the premises, 10,000 square feet off Jermyn Street. I went along and was immediately smitten. The site had been empty for a dozen years or more, but had once been home to the original Quaglino's, a restaurant and night spot that was immensely popular in the 1930s. Boasting royalty among its regulars, the old Quaglino's was also noted for the excellence of its menu – this was not an attribute that was particularly common among British restaurants of the time.

When I made my first visit there, however, history was not uppermost in my mind. The scale of the space was simply breathtaking, dominated by eight massive columns marching down the length of the room and with enough height to insert a mezzanine floor. Here was the perfect opportunity to create a restaurant on a really grand scale – glamorous, buzzing, theatrical – just like La Coupole in Paris.

Getting the lighting right is always critical when it comes to creating the right atmosphere, but at Quaglino's the challenge was particularly great. Our solution was to install a 'skylight' that appears to be toplit by natural light. In fact, above the skylight is not the sky but a car park and several floors of offices. The skylight diffuses artificial lighting which is controlled by a sophisticated computer system to echo natural light levels, bright during the day and mellowing to a sub-fusc tone during the evening. This lighting sleight of hand is to a large extent responsible for the successful realization of that buzzing, brasserie atmosphere that I wanted to create.

Quaglino's has been criticized in some quarters for being noisy. The noise level, however, is quite deliberate. We wanted to pitch the atmosphere in the restaurant somewhere between the raucous clatter of a canteen and the somnolent hush of a temple to gastronomy: Quaglino's was to be a place where people gathered for celebrations, for showing off and for nights on the town. Sartoria, by contrast, our restaurant near Savile Row, has a much quieter atmosphere, and this is achieved with a greater degree of soft furnishing – carpet and upholstered furniture – appropriate for its more intimate, classy quality.

The restaurant at 11 Madison Park is one of my favourites in New York. Designed by Bentel and Bentel, this striking, yet quite simple, room elegantly updates the period interior without being slavishly modern.

Theo Van Doesburg, the maverick Modernist architect and designer, conceived of the Café Aubette in Strasbourg as an exercise in De Stijl colour theory, as the plan makes explicit. The café has been recently restored to its original style by Daniel Gaymard.

Bluebird, London

Fish!, London

St John, London

Converted spaces usually have an industrial feel that's difficult to ignore, and most successful conversions play to the building's original character. Many of them, as here, have one huge advantage over most city-centre locations: volume. At Paci in New York, this has allowed for the introduction of an extra level, whilst at Bluebird we introduced a private dining room up in the eaves, giving the view shown down into the restaurant. With such an imposing shell or environment, it can pay to keep the other elements simple: at St John, one of the first of the new wave of restaurants to open up in Clerkenwell, east London, simple wooden chairs and white-clothed tables complement the space and the gutsy, honest cooking.

Paci, New York

Felix bar and restaurant, Peninsula Hotel, Hong Kong

Belgo Noord, London

Mezzo, London

Kensington Place, London

China Grill, New York

The restaurant as theatre is an idea taken almost to extremes in Philippe Starck's Felix restaurant in Hong Kong, where theatrical canvases act as a backdrop and an audience of chairs awaits the customers. At the original Belgo Noord in north London, designed by Anand Zenz and Ron Arad, guests walk to the restaurant across a twisting path above the kitchen, whilst Mezzo's sweeping staircase affords an equally impressive entrance. Kensington Place, like China Grill in New York, makes the excited talk of customers part of the sense of occasion.

Avenue, London

Circus, London

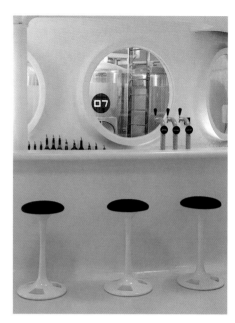

Mash and Air, Manchester

Restaurant bars can be a tough trick to pull off: are they places solely for customers to enjoy an aperitif before eating, or venues in their own right? The answer varies from location to location. The relationship between bar and restaurant at Avenue encourages the transition from drink to food, whereas the 'retro-space age' design of Mash in Manchester is a distinct contrast to Air, the 'grown-up' upstairs restaurant. Bars such as DNA (now redesigned and renamed Marx), above Marco Pierre White's Quo Vadis restaurant in Soho, or Circus, also in Soho, operate as distinct entities, almost entirely independent of the adjacent restaurant.

Light Bar, St Martins Lane Hotel, London

Quo Vadis, London

Zinc Bar & Grill, London

Cantaloupe, London

Tapas bar, Madrid

Everybody craves a genuine local, a place to drop by in the confidence that you'll probably know other people drinking there and where – even if you don't – you are sure of a warm welcome. These are clubs where there's no joining fee and where membership is earned by dint of being a regular. Such spaces as these accrue character over time: there's no point being too precise about where the tables and chairs go, because the whole point is that people will group and re-group them, regulars will stake out their corners and every beer stain tells a story.

Bar, Barbados

Restaurant in Uyuni, Bolivia

Le Pont de la Tour, London

Betty's, Harrogate

Planning the space in the kitchens is as critical as it is at the front-of-house: in a well-run kitchen there is, as the saying goes, a place for everything and everything in its place. One advantage of opening up the kitchen so that it can be seen by people eating in the restaurant or (as with this view of Le Pont de la Tour) to passers-by in the street is that it encourages everyone to take pride in their work and to keep the cooking area spick and span. When the kitchen is in full swing, there's no room for slackness and the ballet of the kitchen is a pleasure to watch.

Kitchen in Tokyo

One H

Le Caprice, London

Social, London

Mash and Air, Manchester

Beddington's, Amsterdam

Beisl-Plutzer Bräu, Spittelberg

Avenue, London

Met Bar, Metropolitan Hotel, London

Stephen Bull's, London

Quality of light can make or break a restaurant, and it can utterly transform it. Le Pont de la Tour turns from a smart business restaurant at lunchtimes to a much softer, more romantic evening venue, a feat we achieve largely by dimming the lights and putting candles on the tables (the riverside setting and views of Tower Bridge help). Le Caprice, like Stephen Bull's, delineates the more public, brightly lit spaces from the subdued, more private tables, whereas Beddington's in Amsterdam is more about light and air.

Mirabelle, London

Odeon, New York

You are never alone with a mirror: every lunchtime and every evening, someone has to be the first customer to arrive, and in bigger spaces, particularly, that can be a lonely and uncomfortable sensation. Strategic use of mirrors can open up views and connect potentially isolated dining spots with the vigour of the main part of the restaurant: for example, the angled mirrors on the walls of Bertorelli's mean that customers facing the wall have something other than their dining partner to look at; whilst the mirrored screens at the entrance to the Mirabelle enhance the glitz of its Mayfair location.

Balthazar, New York

Bertorelli's, London

food & drink

Let fresh flavours speak for themselves. A boiled crab, half a lemon, homemade mayonnaise and freshly baked bread – the best ingredients cooked simply and well.

Without good food, what is a restaurant? To my mind, no amount of intelligent design or charming service can compensate for a meal where the food served is disappointing, lacklustre or pretentious. **Over the last 50 years, there has been an extraordinary increase in our knowledge and appreciation of food:** foreign travel, books, magazines and television have all contributed to this greater awareness. **In Britain, it has long been the case that any decent-sized town will have a fair smattering of Indian and probably Chinese restaurants,** alongside fish and chip bars, teashops and greasy spoons; more recently, these have been joined by bistros and trattorias, pizza parlours and gastro-pubs.

Even in countries where cooking traditions are more firmly established, there are signs of broadening horizons. At the worst extreme, this represents nothing more than the further encroachment of the ubiquitous 'Golden Arches'; at best, an intelligent and enthusiastic re-appraisal of traditional dishes that sensitively updates them using ingredients and cooking techniques borrowed from other cultures. In our global melting pot there is **an abundance of rich and exciting flavours.**

You may find the most wonderful location in the world for your restaurant, you can design the interior and equip the kitchen to perfection, and then employ the most attentive staff, but if the food is atrocious, the entire exercise is meaningless. For customers, the bottom line is what's on the plate. Paying for a meal that one has not enjoyed is an experience most people are reluctant to repeat.

Good food is not all that makes a successful restaurant, but it's the most important part of the 'recipe'. In turn, the quality of a meal is not merely a function of a chef's skill or what goes on in the kitchen. It begins with the quality of the raw materials themselves. To make a great dish you need fresh produce that is full of flavour: no culinary art can ever compensate for second-rate or substandard ingredients.

At the same time, you can have too much of a good thing. Menus need balance. A heavy leaning towards foie gras or truffles can be more off-putting than appetizing. A couple of years ago I visited a restaurant whose chef is considered one of the finest in Europe. Insisting on choosing what we were to eat, he sent out a meal of such richness – three dishes composed of large quantities of foie gras and truffles with everything – that we left the table feeling like we never wanted to eat again. By comparison, the menu at Giradet in Lausanne may comprise seven courses, but the balance is so well judged that afterwards you are left wondering whether you can get in for lunch the next day.

I am a passionate advocate of any cooking style that celebrates the ingredients, that allows the food to speak for itself. Simplicity of approach, a balance of flavours, freshness and good quality raw materials are more likely to create that 'leap in the mouth' that is the hallmark of gastronomic pleasure than any amount of fiddling about with sauces, garnishes and artful presentation. I'm always pleased when a chef has the confidence to serve the great classic dishes, dishes as straightforward as beef bourguignon, roast chicken or grilled dover sole. Nothing is ultimately more satisfying than the best ingredients cooked simply and well.

Fashion and fusion

In days gone by, Paris and Lyons set the culinary standards that were followed by chefs and restaurateurs all over the world. *Haute cuisine*, with its heavy and elaborate sauces and multiplicity of ingredients, represented the peak of culinary perfection for the well-to-do. From New York to London, the language of cooking was French.

In the 1970s, as people grew more concerned about healthy eating, there was a reaction against the old style of classic French cooking. *Nouvelle cuisine*, pioneered by Michel Guérard in his establishments at Eugenie les Bains in south-west France, and in his book *Cuisine Minceur*, represented a radical departure. Guérard is a gifted chef who is passionate about food and cooking. His conception of *nouvelle cuisine* adapted traditional recipes so that they no longer relied on rich, butter- and cream-based sauces, an intelligent interpretation which was both healthy and delicious.

What followed was less commendable. In lesser hands, *nouvelle cuisine* mutated into a ridiculous discipline of minimalist or 'decorated-plate' food: maybe two or three mouthfuls of meat or fish marooned in the middle of a huge plate, embellished with a few artful sprigs of garnish and sitting in a thin puddle of coulis. According to Paul Bocuse, *nouvelle cuisine* 'is a light cooking; the only difficult thing to digest is the bill, which sits heavily on the stomach: the more deserted the plate, the more lavish the bill.' Customers rapidly grew disenchanted with the disparity between the size of their bills and the smallness of their portions.

Today, France has lost its monopoly in the setting of culinary fashions. *Haute* or *nouvelle*, French cooking is but one of many influences that shape restaurant menus today. As more and more people travel, and as they journey further and further afield, influences from Australia, South-east Asia, Japan, the Middle East, Africa and the United States have come into play, leading to entirely new styles of cooking – styles enshrined in those hybrid terms Cal-Ital, Mediterasian and Pacific Rim. 'Fusion' is the new food fashion.

I can admire the confectioner's art, but for me, when food looks too good to eat, there's something wrong. I think mealtimes are, above all else, occasions to enjoy with family and friends: pretentious food can make people uncomfortable because they feel unsure of the etiquette required to eat it.

The basic idea of taking the best from a particular region's culinary repertoire and introducing it at home has much to recommend it. Chinese, Indian and Italian restaurants go back a long way in London; Vietnamese and Moroccan restaurants in Paris; and Indonesian in Amsterdam. Nowhere on earth has such variety as such places as New York, Chicago, San Francisco or Los Angeles, with their rich cultural mix of people. But whereas previously it was necessary to go to a Japanese restaurant to get Japanese food, nowadays, wide-ranging and exotic influences are increasingly making themselves felt within indigenous cooking traditions.

The time was certainly ripe for such an injection of youthful vigour and new trends. These exciting fusion ideas, together with a return to the wholesome and uncomplicated dishes of the Mediterranean, have in fact reinvigorated our whole approach to food in the last decade, from the experience of eating out to what we cook at home. Supermarkets that used to stock only a limited selection of dried herbs and spices now sell quantities of fresh lemongrass, galangal, miso... ingredients most people had never heard of ten or 15 years ago, much less cooked with or tasted. The British, who used to be famous for wanting 'chips with everything' now appear to want 'coriander with everything', if the prevalence of green Thai curry on pub menus is anything to go by.

Quirky combinations, subtle melding of ingredients and surprising mixes can be exciting and refreshing. There are some chefs who can put seemingly unlikely ingredients together with great intelligence and sensitivity. Jean-Georges Vongerichten has been a pioneer of French-Asian cuisine. Jean-Georges, his restaurant in New York, and Vong, in New York and London, really illustrate the attractions of the style. Nobu, after successes in Los Angeles and New York, then opened in London to great acclaim and its unique mix of Japanese cuisine with French and Puerto Rican influences is still hugely popular.

At the same time, it is possible to overdo the originality. In recent years I have seen some quite wonderfully indigestible dishes included on menus – Chocolate Terrine with Curry Anglaise is one that springs to mind. It's always a temptation for young chefs to try and make their mark with something completely different, rather than to stick to the more traditional tried and tested combinations, but it is as well to be aware that, in cooking as in music, there are many more skilled players than there are great composers. 'The discovery of a new dish may well do more for the happiness of mankind than the discovery of a new star', in Brillat-Savarin's famous phrase, but an endless search for novelty can ultimately detract from what is fundamentally a simple pleasure. I'm delighted to see that, in their quest for invention and originality, many chefs have revisited traditional styles of cooking and made use of the marvellous ingredients that are still available from our farms, rivers and coastal waters.

Freshness and flavour

In food, the taste is the thing. One of the most important aspects of a successful restaurant is the quality of the ingredients. All good chefs go to great lengths to ensure that the quality and flavour of the ingredients they use are as good as they can possibly be: if the ingredients are of a high quality, customers are much more likely to get the best possible meal.

Years ago, on one of my first visits to France, I found the markets as inspiring as the restaurants. Unlike supermarkets, where harvest time lasts

There's a fine line between creating an interior that complements the food you intend to serve and making it themed to the point of gimmickry. The New York-based Rockwell group has designed some of the city's most successful restaurants, but I have to say I find the chopstick chairs at Nobu a bit over the top, preferring the more refined interior of Nobu in London's Park Lane.

Japanese food is more dependent on the freshness of the raw ingredients than just about any other cuisine I can call to mind, especially for sushi and sashimi. Tokyo's daily fish market allows restaurants to buy in on a day-to-day basis.

the whole year, in ordinary French food markets what is on offer is what is in season. I really do find it depressing that you can now eat raspberries in January. Doing so removes that pleasant sense of anticipation one used to get in July and the out-of-season fruit tastes nothing like as good as the Scottish raspberries which arrive at the end of September. Many different types of food have a season when they are at their best – asparagus, peas, broad beans and most vegetables and fruit which have a fugitive flavour are best eaten at particular times of the year. The same is true of meat such as lamb and grouse. Even cheeses have a peak time of year. Early summer when the cows have been eating fresh young grass is the time for Brie and Camembert, autumn for Vacherin.

The popular image of the chef getting up at dawn to select fresh produce at the market is largely a myth, certainly in large cities; reputable suppliers of provisions can and do deliver. But markets continue to be a source of inspiration. I know of many chefs who spend a great deal of their holiday time visiting food markets around the world. The great fish markets of Tokyo and Venice, the meat market in Rome where Federico Fellini filmed part of *Roma*, the weekend organic markets at Union Square in New York and on the Boulevard Raspail in Paris are incomparable sources of ideas for flavours and ingredients.

One of the pleasures of shopping daily at a market is that you go with no pre-conceived notions about what you are going to buy. A piece of fresh cod, some baby carrots and a basket of new garlic might inspire you to make an *aoili* that evening. A restaurant menu, of course, requires careful planning, but it is nevertheless important to retain the same sense of seasonality and be able to respond creatively to what is available and fresh.

A chef has a much better opportunity to buy good quality produce than the ordinary consumer. Although the quality and variety of food available in supermarkets and shops has improved considerably, there is an inevitable time lag – vegetables will not get into the shops the day, or even the day after, they are picked, and fish is possibly two days out of water before it reaches the counter. If a chef has a good relationship with a fishmonger they can get freshly caught seafood, shellfish and freshwater fish within 12 hours, brought directly to the kitchen.

Vegetables, if flown in, will probably have arrived in the country the day before they get to the restaurant kitchen, thus not losing all their flavour as so often happens when they are exposed to long periods in a chilled or gas-filled environment. If they are home-grown they will very likely arrive in the restaurant kitchen the day they are harvested. During its season, English asparagus, which has a notoriously fugitive flavour, is cut at dawn and delivered to our restaurants by 10 a.m. the same morning.

In the summer months our restaurants make good use of my herb garden in Berkshire – twice a week the chefs fax their orders to the head gardener, he cuts bunches of tarragon, marjoram, parsley, lovage or basil and despatches them to London, arriving within six hours. There is often a surfeit of artichokes, courgettes, runner beans and pumpkins, all of which go straight to our kitchens. We grow potatoes specially for some of the chefs – ratte and pink fir apple, delicious and waxy, are the most popular varieties. Unusual salad leaves such as mizuna, purslane, rocket and claytonia are grown in Essex for the restaurants, arriving the same day they are picked. It is very unusual for the domestic consumer to be able to buy produce this fresh.

On the other hand, meat and game needs long hanging to develop its flavour and texture. Very often supermarkets sell meat that is underhung; it looks appealing, uniform in colour and texture, but the flavour is just not there. A chef, however, will look for beef with a dark colour and yellowish fat. Scottish Angus is superlative beef, expensive but of such consistent quality it never lets a chef down. After the BSE scare and with fewer people eating beef, we felt it important to be able to find a source that came from certified herds with no history of the disease. We found just such a supplier in Ireland, a cooperative of beef farmers that slaughter their own cattle and will butcher the meat to the cuts demanded by our chefs.

Chickens present another challenge, with the bulk of what is available being battery-produced. At present, the best birds come from France, the *poulet de Bresse* and *label rouge* are free-range and grain-fed. Improvements are gradually being made in poultry production in Britain: what's required is to choose breeds that are slow-growing and rear them in open surroundings, allowing them to feed as naturally as possible with as much space as possible. This is how the premium-priced Bresse birds are reared, why they have much better flavour and why they are relatively expensive. They really do taste as a chicken should – vastly different from the insipid, flavourless poultry commonly offered in supermarkets, which, if it tastes of anything, tastes of fishmeal.

Good chefs travel as much as they can and eat out in others' restaurants at every opportunity. Many of them, too, like to work in other restaurants on their days off and in their holidays. All of this broadens their experience, exposes them to different foods and methods of cooking, and they often come back to their kitchens ready to make a change. It may be a different variety of pepper they ate in Italy or some mushrooms they tasted in Boston, and they want to put them on the menu. I was in Stockholm a few years ago and had dinner in a restaurant where we ate really wonderful potatoes. After the meal the chef came out and I asked him about the potatoes. He didn't know the variety, he thought they came from Lapland, but he kindly gave me a little bag of them. I took them to our gardener who let them sprout. They were planted and the next year we had about two dozen of these delicious potatoes, half of which we ate, the others we left to sprout for replanting. We still don't know the variety, so they are tagged 'Stockholm' in the garden and every year we get a slightly bigger crop.

What's on the menu

When you are considering opening a restaurant it is very important to decide on the type of food you expect to serve. Always look for a gap in the market, don't just copy the food that some other restaurant is successfully serving. It is worth being pioneering with your menu. Just because an area has 20 Indian restaurants, it does not follow that local people will only eat curries. Look for your own speciality – something that you cook particularly well yourself or something that your chef is passionate about and experienced in cooking.

After we have appointed a chef, we spend quite a lot of time discussing the type of restaurant, the sort of menu, the price range and the type of customers we expect. We usually start with a long list of recipes that we believe are right for the particular project. We talk at length about the dishes we know sell well in our other restaurants, how long or short the menu should be and the current trends in food and cooking in general. We know from the experience we have gained in our other restaurants that we sell more fish than meat, that offal is considered a sophisticated taste and is consequently difficult to sell, and that people like to choose a vegetable accompaniment rather than have it provided for them on the plate. (I've always wanted to open a restaurant specializing in one of my favourite types of food – offal – but I suspect it would be a financial failure.) It's then up to the chef to come up with a proposed menu based on these original ideas and arrange a tasting session.

At the outset it is also important to bear in mind the change in the customer base from lunchtime through to the evening. If you have a large residential catchment, the evening trade may not be on the same economic footing as the customers who will come during the working day, generally wanting to eat in under an hour, and it may be necessary to adjust the prices and the menu accordingly.

One way of coming up with a menu is to base it on dishes you have eaten and enjoyed in another country. Many restaurants have found their niche serving what for the want of a better term might be called 'ethnic cooking'. Belgo, for instance, brought the Belgian tradition of eating mussels and chips and drinking handmade beers to London; Michael Chow took Chinese food upmarket by serving it in sophisticated surroundings and employing charming Italian waiters; Peter Boizot saw a gap in the market for proper Italian pizza; Momo became an overnight success with its souk-like interior and authentic Moroccan food.

Another way to fill a gap in the market is to specialize in cooking which relies heavily on a particular type of ingredient. Marco Pierre White has sensed that foie gras and truffles are luxuries people will pay for; I saw that crustacea rarely featured on restaurant menus in London; the River Café

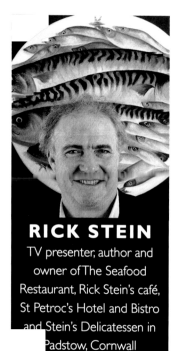

RICK STEIN

TV presenter, author and owner of The Seafood Restaurant, Rick Stein's café, St Petroc's Hotel and Bistro and Stein's Delicatessen in Padstow, Cornwall

" Just the other day I was looking at the books from our first year, 1975, and saw that what we made in a year we now take in a day. My wife Jill and I had one smallish restaurant on the quayside in Padstow, specializing in fish and seafood, and in those days places like Cornwall were not really on the gastronomic map. One of the things I felt I had to do to get the restaurant known and taken seriously was to write a book about fish, not from any budding desire to be an author, but as a promotional tool. It wasn't just my restaurant that needed promoting, but the whole idea of eating fish. I remember talking to a friend at the publishers Penguin and idly saying that I reckoned I could write a book. Three weeks later she rang to say the cookery editor wanted me to do an outline.

The opportunity to make a television series came quite soon after the book was published. I met the director with whom I subsequently worked when the TV-chef Keith Floyd came to our restaurant and filmed a short piece with me. My first two television series were both based in Padstow and the result was incredible – our business probably doubled. It has calmed down now, which is good because it got to the point where our old customers couldn't get in.

I really enjoyed my time cooking six days a week but as I started to get older, and particularly as the business got quite big, I became tired. In my mid-forties I was wondering if there was any way out. It wasn't that I didn't still feel very enthusiastic about the job, but I started to get really annoyed at the effort it required. There are people a lot older than me who still do work that hard, but I decided to move on and am now more the director of a business than a chef. And it is a very exciting career move for me. We have proper managers and financial controllers working for us, which is fun. I don't cook nearly as much as I used to, but I still write the recipes, oversee the menu and work on quality control. I spend a lot of time in the kitchen when I'm here, watching what the chefs are cooking, advising and demonstrating.

The challenge now is to maintain the style, atmosphere and commitment to the sort of food we like. As long as you can make sure the staff do exactly what you want, or – better still – learn to do things exactly as you do, it's fine. Consistency problems come when you open a chain of restaurants and the business becomes corporate. Our two smaller restaurants are subsidiaries or satellites, not reproductions of the original.

The next step for us in the future is to plan and set up a cooking school for training aspiring chefs, which is going to be really taxing. We want it to be very good and will put all our chefs through it. "

has now established a wonderful reputation for robust Italian food; Antonio Carluccio specializes in funghi, Fish! specializes in what you would expect. Specialization, which offers the customer an element of pre-selection, can be very attractive.

Alternatively, inspiration can come from a cooking method. Many restaurants have menus based on the type of cooking that results from using a rotisserie, wood-fired oven, charcoal grill, wok, tandoor oven or smokebox. At Bluebird, for example, one of the features of the kitchen is a wood-fired oven; accordingly, the menu includes a variety of wood-roasted dishes such as pigeon, rabbit, cod and vegetables.

While the location of the restaurant, the type of customers you are likely to attract and the price range will all dictate the menu to some extent, the final decision should rely on experience and gut instinct. When we were approached to create a restaurant in the landmark development at Number One Poultry in the City of London, I felt that a classic Burgundian cuisine mixed with northern French dishes would do very well there. Most of the diners would be businesspeople from the City, and I believed they would welcome a return to classic food, which, when done well, can still outshine the Pacific Rim and the fusion cooking we have seen so much of in the past five years. Burgundy is a rich source of fabulous chicken recipes, which seemed particularly appropriate for a restaurant called Coq d'Argent. The chef was briefed and together we had a wonderful time going through French recipe books, revisiting old favourites such as Elizabeth David, Richard Olney, Julia Child, Simone Beck and especially Bernard Oiseau.

When we found another site in Savile Row, a rather plain but handsome building, I immediately thought it should be a Milanese restaurant. At that time London had several excellent Italian restaurants serving the wonderful rustic dishes of Tuscany and Umbria, but I wanted to have something different, something cool and urban. The menu at Sartoria therefore has

classic northern Italian dishes such as costolette and risotto alla Milanese, simple grilled fish and pastas, served in a quiet, refined and sophisticated interior.

Naturally enough, what's on the menu has an important bearing on the way the kitchen is designed, which means that the chef has to work in close partnership with the architect and kitchen designer from the beginning. A restaurant that is serving classic contemporary food will require specific storage and preparation space for the high quality seasonal meat and fish, vegetables and fruit on the menu. An Italian restaurant requires different arrangements for keeping olive oils, pastas, cured meats and cheeses and may need specialist equipment such as pasta makers and brick ovens. In restaurants specializing in crustacea, you need facilities to cook live shellfish, blast-chill them, then keep them cold. In cafés serving lighter menus, with salads, cold dishes and a couple of pasta specials each day, kitchens may require a grill, rotisserie and pasta cooking equipment.

Sourcing

Sourcing ingredients is one of the most important parts of putting a menu together. In this respect, chefs should maintain good relationships with suppliers so that they can depend on the quality of the produce and its constant availability. Patronizing local producers of cheese, herbs, vegetables, chickens or eggs, for example, can be advantageous all round – ensuring a consistent supply for the chef and a ready market for the producer.

Seasonal produce, such as grouse, English asparagus and wild salmon, which has the best flavour, can carry a premium price. Likewise, carefully reared livestock or organically produced vegetables and fruit tend to cost very much more and are not always available. In a small restaurant, the chef can write the menu from day to day, based on availability and price of

This, to me, is one of the most appetizing sights there is, a plate of seasonal vegetables, plucked from the earth, scrubbed, boiled (where necessary) and served: wholesome, generous, healthy and simple.

ingredients. There may be a glut of asparagus, a particularly fine crop of raspberries or the conditions might be just right for a good supply of shellfish. Such factors can bring the price of otherwise costly ingredients down: expensive ingredients impart a certain sense of generosity to the menu.

In a larger restaurant, it is more difficult to be quite so flexible. While the idea of going to market and writing the menu daily is utterly appealing, it is not practical for big enterprises that demand more forward planning; in such cases, purchasing inevitably has to be rationalized. In 1995, after a time of rapid expansion, we appointed a purchasing director for the Conran restaurants and he was given the brief to implement a total overhaul of the existing purchasing functions and to set up an efficient department whose ultimate responsibility was to buy all staple products and negotiate prices for fresh produce. This was quite a job. Until then the purchasing department had consisted solely of a manager and a junior assistant; there were no systems in place, which in turn meant there was no historical data available. At that time we were buying ingredients for some 10,000 meals a day.

The new purchasing director saw it was vital that some sort of centralization was established in order to optimize efficiency. With different individuals previously acting as buyers, discrepencies had been rife and there were some cases of suppliers quoting quite contrasting prices to different Conran restaurants for exactly the same product.

As well as negotiating the prices for all the food, our purchasing department manages the contracts and oversees the supply chain, from the supplier or manufacturer to delivery direct to the restaurants. The department also has to ensure that the agreed specifications are maintained, the costs remain constant within reason, deliveries are on time and provide monthly reports on spending for the accountants.

This terrine is a testimony to the patience and skill of the chef, but it's not so over-complicated that you wonder why anyone would bother.

Although the purchasing department of Conran restaurants has acquired a great deal of experience, has formed excellent contacts with suppliers and now has fairly hefty buying clout, individual chefs are also encouraged to take an active role in finding the produce they need for their restaurants. Central buying makes sense when it comes to purchasing staples – flour, oils, salt – and can have a real impact on negotiating price, but it is important that a chef has the final say on the quality of food.

The art of buying is a question of achieving the right balance between financial expediency and individual flair or preference. The department regularly holds blind-tasting sessions where the head chefs get together, sample a range of produce and give their opinions, the reasons why something is particularly good, and why something else may be unacceptable. This dialogue between buyers and chefs is important – it informs the buyers of the quality the chefs expect and the chefs are exposed to a breadth of produce that they may not otherwise experience. There is an increasing trend towards sourcing high quality produce from small suppliers and setting up partnerships allowing the restaurant to have an exclusive supply. We have several products that are grown or gathered specially for us. Many other restaurants operate in the same way; Pizza Express have imported all the ingredients for their pizzas from Italy since they started, which certainly gives them a quality advantage over their competitors.

When our chef began work at Mezzo and Mezzonine, he had to seek out suppliers of south-east Asian products that were rarely found in Britain in those days. This involved spending time hanging around outside shops and restaurants in Chinatown waiting to accost delivery men who might be able to introduce him to the right people. Another source of supply turned out to be the shops favoured by his Asian kitchen staff, retailers who were importing products on a small scale for their own businesses. The chef did not manage to get all the ingredients he wanted for the menu until a few months after opening; but the popularity of the dishes at Mezzo and Mezzonine proved to be evidence of a shift in taste which has now seen south-east Asian ingredients becoming more widely available in British supermarkets.

Pricing

Food costs are an element that can make or break a restaurant. The gross profit, that which is left when you take the buying cost away from the selling price, needs to be high enough to sustain the various other expenses incurred in running a restaurant – the administration, the wages, rent, light, heat, advertising, furniture replacement, laundry and a myriad of other things. These expenses need to be stringently controlled so that the net profit ends up as close to the gross profit as possible. In order to be financially successful, a restaurant really needs to make about a 70 per cent gross profit, and to achieve this it is essential to get the best possible prices for produce of the highest possible quality.

When we have fine-tuned the dishes, eliminated some that we don't think will sell and added others that we know will, the cost controller takes the menu and the detailed specifications for each dish and comes up with an accurate cost per dish. The costing has to consider absolutely everything – salt and pepper, the amount of oil or butter used in cooking, the potential wastage, portion size and even the complimentary bread and butter on the table.

Menus not only have to be balanced from an aesthetic point of view, but also in terms of costing. Fish is more expensive to buy than vegetables, so the margin will be lower. Puddings and pasta dishes, whose basic ingredients are largely inexpensive, can achieve relatively high margins. And then you have to remember that for every 100 main courses, there are likely to be 90 starters and coffees, 150 side dishes, but only 50 puddings sold. To get the figures to work demands juggling the number of low-cost/high-margin/low-volume dishes on the menu with the number of high-cost/low-margin/high-volume dishes.

Once the prices have been preliminarily established, it is also important to consider the competition. How many starters, main courses and puddings do other restaurants, either in the locality or further afield, have on the menu, what are their prices and are items such as bread or a cover charge included? Looking at the competition in this way may give you a good indication of whether or not you have done your sums correctly. If your restaurant is significantly cheaper than your main rivals, consider the idea that you may be underselling yourself. If you are wildly more expensive, you risk pricing yourself out of the market and making nothing at all.

Controlling wastage is a key element in keeping food costs down. The implications can be staggering: if £70 worth of food is wasted at a service, it can add up to about £1,000 per week or £50,000 a year. When a new chef took over at Bluebird, one of the dishes on the menu was wood-roast rabbit, but only the saddle and hind quarters were being used; the rest of the rabbit was being thrown away. The new chef immediately put *rillettes de lapin*, made with the fore legs and skirt, on the menu, used the carcass to make stock and gravy, and the livers to make a pâté that was offered as a special. Similarly, he now buys whole ducks and uses the breast for one dish, makes the legs into confit, which he stores, puts the wing tips into stock and uses the carcass to make a broth. The chickens on the rotisserie that are not ordered during the lunch service go towards making

By contrast, all of us from time to time enjoy generous portions of comfort food.

a delicious salad for the evening. Minimum wastage is not the only benefit of this kind of practice: it can be educational for many of the younger kitchen staff, who do not always realize where a fillet of beef comes from, how a salmon fits back together, or that streaky bacon comes from belly pork.

However, there are occasions when the labour costs outweigh the benefits of using every bit of food and certainly one should never sacrifice quality just to use every last scrap. For example, a lot of restaurants no longer buy whole chickens, and in recent times it has been hard to use a whole side of beef – largely because there was a restriction on using the bones, that had previously used in stockpots in every kitchen in the land.

The chefs at Quaglino's initially peeled and cut their own chips, some 450kg per day, all of which had to be stored and then fried off. Preparing and cooking the chips alone was demanding a disproportionate amount of labour and it was very difficult in such a large restaurant to guarantee consistent quality every time. After extensive testing, the chefs switched to buying fresh, ready-cut chips from our vegetable supplier, who set up a peeling and cutting service for us using the best quality potatoes which he buys in bulk. Similarly, at Bluebird, where 2½ tonnes of chips regularly come out of the kitchens in the period between Friday to Sunday, making the chips from scratch would be a logistical nightmare. At Le Pont de la Tour, where the demand for chips is much smaller, the chefs cut all their own chips and have always done so.

Each chef has to make their own decision about what is right for their kitchen. Among the Conran restaurants, Mezzo buys in pasta, while Bluebird makes all its own; Bluebird buys in tomato juice but not canned tomatoes, because the chefs feel there are enough good varieties around now always to use fresh ones.

One of the great headaches for a chef – and one of the great skills – is knowing how much to order and cook for each dish in each service. Of course, it comes down to experience, but there are given formulae to help in the assessment of quantities. A general rule of thumb is that a chef should stay within the limit of spending one-third of the previous day's takings. It is a bit simplistic, but the formula works and won't get a chef into financial difficulties – in the short term!

We have developed a menu pack for each of our restaurants' kitchens. This gives detailed descriptions of and recipes for every dish on each menu, which facilitates the *mise en place* and ordering. It means that a dish is prepared and cooked the same way every time, ensuring consistency. And it makes it easy to keep a check on the costs and, therefore, the margins. At our new restaurant in Manhattan we are going one better and taking a digital photograph of each dish so that all the necessary information appears on the screen at the click of a mouse. A chef needs to know at any time the value of the stock he is holding and his menu costings. Such attention to detail can mean the difference between a restaurant's success or failure.

An additional problem for very large restaurants such as Bluebird, which has three kitchens and a foodstore, is that with so much produce arriving, it is sometimes difficult to keep an eye on quality – occasionally a consignment of herbs in a tired state gets accepted, or a crate of turbot that are too small. We implemented a system whereby for four weeks the chefs of the relevant sections were called to the delivery bay to inspect the goods coming in. This gave the goods-in staff the training and knowledge of what is acceptable or not and, while it may have been tiresome for the chefs at the beginning, the end result was better quality produce coming into the kitchens in the long term.

The cellar at La Tour d'Argent in Paris is home to one of the finest, most extensive and most expensive wine lists in the capital.

OLIVER PEYTON

Owner of Gruppo Limited, including the Atlantic Bar and Grill, Coast, Mash and Air and Isola

The bar culture is very important to restaurants today, and this is true whether you are talking about cocktails or beer. In Britain there is a new generation of restaurant-goers who have travelled widely, eaten out and drunk in other countries. They know that in Madrid, for example, an evening out doesn't even start until 10 or 11 p.m., and they want to stay out late back at home, too. People want more than a single experience when they go out for an evening, and a lot of traditional restaurants have not offered that in the past. Now, however, the London cocktail culture is as strong as that in New York; if anything I feel London increasingly offers more creativity and a wider range of drinks. The British are up for anything.

Sixty per cent of our company's sales are based on alcoholic drinks, including drinks with meals and pre- and after-dinner drinks. The Atlantic Bar and Grill in London has a huge bar, averaging 1,800 people through the doors each night, 500 of whom will take dinner. It is the largest retailer of Tattinger in the world, sells 1,600 martinis per week and 600 caipirinhas. We have two full-time trainers just for the bar staff.

With the launch of Mash, which has two branches brewing four beers at any one time, we wanted to prove that you can make good beer in England, and that in order to enjoy it you do not have to go and stand in a 'spit and sawdust' pub. In Mash, people drinking beer sit next to people drinking champagne, and there is no stigma attached to any particular drink. We also offer 60 cocktails, two types of coffee, an extensive wine list and freshly pressed juices.

We cater to a mind-set rather than a group based on age, culture or class. I find there is very little difference between our customers in Manchester and London, although in Manchester people are more likely to drink beer because they have had less exposure to quality cocktails. And 50 per cent of the trade in Manchester is on Friday and Saturday nights because people tend not to live in the city centre so they go home and then come back into town for a night out.

Today, people are generally exposed to the same media all over the world. Thirty-five per cent of our business is tourist. London is now a major travel destination and when our restaurants feature in international magazines we attract a lot of business. However, we try to avoid the risk of being famous for 15 minutes and try to do things that don't date: it's possible to be interesting and classic at the same time. You can't fool the public. It's quality that keeps people coming back.

The wine list

A good restaurant is inevitably judged as much by its wine list as by its menu. Achieving the right balance of wines is important – between Burgundies and Bordeaux, between European and New World wines, between inexpensive and costly. The wine list should be based largely upon the type of customers the restaurant expects to attract. For example, there is little point in putting a large number of rare vintages on the list for a casual Mediterranean-style restaurant, or a bar and grill which is offering good-value food and quick service.

The size of the list can also be important. Small but interesting wine lists appeal more to customers, who often find long lists intimidating. When faced with a list of biblical proportions, a diner will tend to opt for something that sounds familiar – Sancerre and Chablis are good sellers for this reason, while Echezeaux rarely sells because customers find it hard to pronounce the name. The best-selling wine in Quaglino's and Mezzo is a Chablis, with Sancerre coming in at third place, following the house champagne. Seasonality obviously affects customers' choices as well, with the lighter white wines far outselling reds in hot summers, and full-bodied reds popular in winter months.

Our wine department has had to expand enormously in the past five years and over this time it has been radically upgraded. Originally the department had a dedicated buyer who not only selected the wines, but also set the selling prices, had sole authorization of the invoices and the contract negotiations. As a result of the expansion of the wine-buying function, this arrangement was perceived as placing far too much responsibility on one individual.

The wine buying for our restaurants is done centrally, and is overseen by our consultant Bill Baker, who works for us three days a week. There is also a considerable amount of input from the sommeliers in each restaurant, who know which wines are likely do well with their individual customers. Our centralized list now features some 950 wines. These are divided into three categories: the core stock, those selling at £14 to £25, which represent 80 per cent of our sales; the premium wines priced at £25 to £50; and fine wines, those in excess of £50. Again it is important to have a good balance within the price ranges as there is a higher turnover in the core stock, which also attracts a higher margin. Together, our restaurants sell about 20,000 bottles a week, which gives us a significant buying clout. Each restaurant will require a different mix of price ranges, vintages, producers and countries of origin. The list at Sartoria, for instance, which has a predominately Italian menu, consists of a total of 252 Italian wines – a range that is one of the most comprehensive in London.

Whilst this purchasing organization may seem bureaucratic, its presence is justified for a large-ish collection of restaurants. Its responsibilities are indicative, however, of the scale of work that must be undertaken to maintain a wine list for a smaller restaurant.

Writing the list is a skill in itself. Notes are useful, and not only for the customer's information: they can be of real benefit in staff training. It's not always practical to make notes on every wine, but a brief indication of the region or variety is helpful. Bill Baker's passion for wines is palpable. People have been known to keep a copy of his wine list on their bedside tables; it is an amusing, enjoyable and informative read. He puts together the lists for Conran restaurants with deftness and sensitivity, balancing the prices, the vintages and the varieties to each of the restaurants' demands.

Buying wine involves tasting, tasting and tasting. Visiting vineyards, talking to producers, negociants, merchants and dealers is also part of the process, but tasting is the key. The widely held belief that you will never get a bad wine from a good producer can encourage a tendency to verticality in a list. While 18 consecutive vintages from one producer on a list can look very impressive, it is necessary to be very confident of the source.

Purchasing fine wines in particular demands an enormous amount of investment up front, but invariably the return gained from the sale of fine wines balances the capital tied up in the stock. We carry about a quarter of a million pounds worth of fine wine stock.

Wine also takes up a huge amount of space. In our case, the bulk of our wine is stored in cellar conditions away from the restaurants, with orders delivered as they are needed. Knowing how much stock to keep chilled for immediate consumption is down to experience. When we first opened Mezzo the weather was unseasonably warm and it seemed that every diner ordered white wine – chilling the stocks quickly enough was a big headache expecially as bottled waters and beers also had to be cold.

The job of sommelier embraces many facets other than simply pouring wine. While a small restaurant with a well-chosen list might find it difficult to justify the expense of this particular member of staff, the sommelier can be quite invaluable in larger establishments. Even if you are going to do without a sommelier, it is still essential for someone take an interest in and responsibility for the wine.

There's something intrinsically appealing about a well-stocked bar. Perhaps it is simply the comforting knowledge that you are in an establishment where the owner or manager cares passionately about his or her business.

Stocktaking, done once a month, is one of the sommelier's most important jobs, but it is no longer the laborious task it used to be of counting bottles and cases. Now computers can provide an instant read-out of what has been bought, sold, and where the wine is – in the cellars, in the restaurant, in bond or waiting to be shipped.

Another key task is to look after the wine, which includes planning the layout of the cellar. When wine arrives at a restaurant it must be checked to ensure that the order is complete, the vintages are correct and that it is in good condition. Then the bottles have to be racked and stored in temperature-controlled conditions. Stocks have to be kept up, not just of wines but water, liqueurs, cognacs, gin, vodka, beers, mixers and any other drink – all of this so-called 'wet stock' is also the sommelier's responsibility.

But the central – and the most rewarding and enjoyable – part of a sommelier's job is selling wine to the customer. To recommend a wine, it is essential to know what it tastes like. Sommeliers must also be familiar with the menu, and know which wines would complement a dish or combination of dishes. They must be able to talk to their customers, advise, recommend and lead them in their choices. Few people are all that knowledgable about wine and most appreciate some guidance, especially when it comes to wines from less familiar areas. At Sartoria, for instance, the sommelier is of vital importance because most of the customers have never encountered some of the Italian wines on our list.

Our sommelier at Bluebird Club reports that the members are increasingly willing to make use of his knowledge and skill, asking for recommendations, discussing the menu and the choices he can offer. Younger customers, in particular, seem keen to seek advice.

Several of our sommeliers are active members of the British Sommeliers' Club, set up several years ago as an offshoot of the French association. They meet once a month for tastings and tutorials. Wine merchants, not unnaturally, are very keen to host these tastings – it is a great boon to a merchant to get his wines on a good list with a high turnover. London is the greatest wine market in the world and producers want their wines on the lists of as many of London's prestige restaurants as possible. Increasingly, wine suppliers help restaurateurs to compile and write their wine lists, and as this is seen as a way of adding value to the merchant's service, they do not attempt to restrict the restaurateur to one supplier.

Asparagus grower   **Chocolate maker from Lyon**   **Bresse chicken farmer**   **Man with langouste from Brittany**

Toby Glanville's portraits, displayed in Coq d'Argent, connect us with those who fish, farm, bake or make the ingredients and food that ends up on our plates.

Ham curer Fish grader from Penzance Oysterman Olive stuffer from Collioure

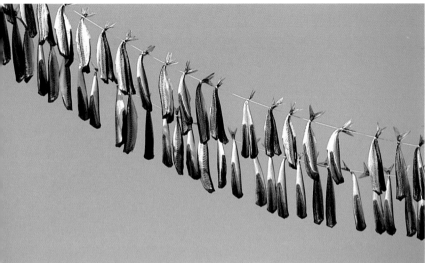

Sundried anchovies from Spain

Fish in Kwangjang market, Seoul

Depending on the scale of operations, setting up your own restaurant may entail daily trips to the market; even if that luxury is not an option, daily deliveries of fresh produce are essential, as is rigorous checking in, to ensure both the quality and quantity are up to standard.

Market in Lebanon

Fishmonger, Quai des Belges, Marseilles

The Cow, London

Beach meal, Antibes

Simple pleasures: a plateau of fruits de mer shared with friends,
with the obligatory pint of Guinness, of course; or alternatively
a croque monsieur and a tumbler *à pression*, a pizza and a glass
of wine, bread and cheese or a couple of *gelati* to share. Snack
foods are about the spur of the moment, and have an
honourable history.

Caffè Florian, Venice

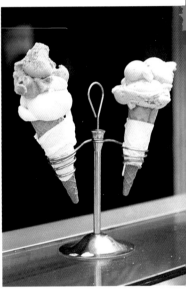

Gelati, Venice

Hotel Mongeto, near Turin

As the adage goes – you are what you eat. National stereotypes aside (and the Frenchman with his block of Camembert is a piece of German propaganda), we increasingly associate different diets with lifestyle choices, whether it's 'think thin, be beautiful' or 'eat, drink and be merry', the rallying cry of the bon viveur.

Fish restaurant, Fukuoka

French bistro

A Vietnamese imperial banquet, Huopong Giang

Floating market, Bangkok

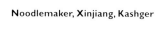

The last 50 years have seen the globalization of the kitchen. Whether on holiday abroad or in their home town, people are increasingly adventurous about the food they eat. New ingredients and new cooking techniques are shared and exchanged at increasing speed. But what expense authenticity: can you really blame Mr and Mrs Middle England for feeling so embarrassed at being dressed up for a 'traditional' Vietnamese banquet?!

Noodlemaker, Xinjiang, Kashger

Lamb kebabs, Morocco

Italian sushi, Swiss Centre, Milan – truly an example of mixed metaphor!

Raw blowfish, Kozue, Park Hyatt Hotel, Tokyo

The way that food is presented on a plate could occupy the pages of a book in itself. With presentation comes all sorts of expectations: to me, the time that's been invested simply arranging the pieces of lobster on to a plate in the kitchens at the Grand Véfour can never justify absurd prices. But that is not to say that I think food should just be slopped on a plate, without regard for how it looks. And, just to contradict myself, I find one of the pleasures of visiting Japan to be the rigorous formality and attention to detail in a formal kaiseki meal; but many people, I am sure, would find the picture of skewered sweetfish the most challenging of the dishes here if they were presented with it in a restaurant.

Salt grilled sweetfish, Kozue, Park Hyatt Hotel, Tokyo

Grand aïoli, in my opinion a perfect dish

Seared scallops with truffled potatoes, Rubicon, San Francisco

Never serve oysters *in a month that has no paycheck in it.*

P J O'ROURKE

Homard aux artichauts, Grand Véfour, Paris

Coffee house, Canberra

English afternoon tea at Peak Lounge, Park Hyatt Hotel, Tokyo

Betty's, Harrogate

Café Gandolfi, Glasgow

Tea-time around the world shows up shared values and differences. From egg-and-cress sandwiches at Betty's in Harrogate to silver service in Tokyo (from waitresses dressed by Issey Miyake), tea is a meal that combines the casual with the ritualistic. Should the crusts be cut from sandwiches, and are they triangles or squares? Is the espresso of a suitably tar-like consistency, the froth of the cappuccino creamy enough? Consistency and attention to detail always pay off.

I look upon it that he **who does not mind his belly** *will hardly mind anything else.*

SAMUEL JOHNSON

Parisian café

service

At Chartier in Paris, it's not just food and wine stains on the tablecloth that record what you've had to eat.

Restaurant staff are the human face of the business and they bring the place to life. Having said this, good service does not happen by magic: staff always need to be well trained and thoroughly briefed; they need to feel confident about what they are doing, and to understand the roles of their colleagues. They also need to be able to work under pressure: **a restaurant in full swing is an incredibly busy place,** and everything needs to be timed to perfection.

In France, where food and restaurants have always been treated with respect, **working in a restaurant has long been a reputable occupation.** Elsewhere (and especially in English-speaking countries) it has, until recently, been viewed as a rather dead-end job. Fortunately, times have changed, and **the restaurant business is, these days, seen as a glamorous and rewarding career.** However, never forget that this business is also incredibly hard work! Nonetheless, good staff are still at a premium, and **half the battle these days is holding on to them by keeping them involved, interested and challenged** in the everyday running of the restaurant and in their long-term career there.

Of the three principal elements that go towards the making of a successful restaurant, service is the most ephemeral. Once you have chosen a location and come up with a spatial design, the physical fabric of the restaurant is a constant, give or take wear and tear. The food, too, should not vary to an appreciable degree after the chef has established a menu, set up the kitchen and nutured good relationships with suppliers. But the staff – everyone from the maître d'hotel to the waiters, sommeliers and receptionists – are more or less free agents. After each service they walk out of the door, and unless they come back the restaurant will not survive. And they do walk out: in 1998 the restaurant trade had a staff turnover of 40 per cent.

The most striking of transformations that have taken place in the restaurant business in recent years, most notably in Britain, but elsewhere in the world as well, has been the change in the way restaurants are viewed as employers. It was not long ago that many restaurant jobs were regarded as dead-ends or stop-gaps. Serving drinks, checking coats, taking bookings, waiting tables or working behind the scenes in the kitchen were seen solely as short-term occupations for students earning extra money in the holidays, backpackers working their way round the globe, actors 'resting' between parts – or those lacking both ambition and more formal skills. The work was generally casual, fairly badly paid, and poorly managed and administered. Training was cursory; career structure minimal; and conditions ranged from the substandard to the downright hellish. George Orwell's *Down and Out in Paris and London* may have been written before the war, but the typically squalid working environments the book portrays have taken many years to disappear from the scene.

Service, as we are constantly reminded, is the new growth sector of the economy, overtaking manufacturing in many developed countries. This factor alone has not been responsible for the rise in status of restaurant work; equally important have been changing attitudes within the industry itself, which is increasingly run on a more professional basis than ever before.

Restaurants today, particularly the larger establishments, provide an impressively wide range of employment opportunities, both semi-skilled and highly professional: buyers to source food, wine and other elements; accountants to oversee running costs, purchasing accounts, VAT returns, credit card receipts and profit or loss margins; personnel managers to hire and fire; PR to arrange publicity. Supervising all this activity means that there has to be a sound management structure to administer what can be two complete sets of staff for a restaurant that trades seven days and seven nights a week.

There is career scope for entry at all levels, from chef to kitchen porter, from cloakroom attendant to purchasing director. And within the trade itself there is immense mobility as staff move up the ladder, taking their skills and training from restaurant to restaurant or from tier to tier within the same organization. Restaurant work now offers the chance to fashion a lifelong career.

Training and recruitment

For the first-time restaurateur, staff selection and training can cause a great many headaches. One of the side-effects of the increasing number of restaurants opening here in London has been a growing shortage of good chefs and waiters. Like any profession, the restaurant world has its own bush

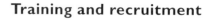
A young waiter from Enna, in Sicily.

telegraph and word soon gets out when there are new job opportunities for staff between jobs or those looking to make a change. Nevertheless, it is an unwritten law that one should never directly attempt to poach the staff of another establishment. Recruitment can be done through agencies, but these vary in terms of professionalism; the worst make no attempt to check qualifications and you may end up employing chefs with total ignorance of the most basic cooking techniques. On the confident recommendation of employment agencies, we have interviewed chefs de partie who confessed that they did not know how to make a bearnaise sauce, one of the most basic qualifications in a chef's progression to *gros bonnet*.

It is far more reliable to look for staff with certified levels of training. Just after the war, the Westminster Technical College set up a programme to train chefs and waiters, a significant element of which was a restaurant where staff could exercise their talents on real paying customers, who would offer both the praise and criticism one might expect in a bona fide restaurant. In a guide to London published in 1952, the college's restaurant was featured as offering lunch consisting of smoked salmon, apricot pie and coffee, all for the exceptionally reasonable price of 3s 6d. Today, The Vincent Room, which is still run by the college, is well patronized by the office workers of Victoria who consider its three courses for under a tenner pretty much of a bargain.

We took a leaf out of the same book when we decided to found the Butlers Wharf Chef School, partly in self-interest to address the shortage of good staff, and partly in acknowledgement of our responsibility, as employers of large numbers of such people, of exacerbating to some extent

that shortage in the first place. The idea was welcomed and encouraged by the London Docklands Development Corporation, Southwark Council, The Hotel and Catering Training Company, as well as some of London's leading restaurateurs. A key element of the chef school is The Apprentice, a restaurant open to the public which serves as an environment where trainée chefs and front-of-house staff can practise on paying customers. The Apprentice has proved to be very popular, offering food cooked by young chefs that is then served by rather hesitant novice waiters, often on their first day in the job, and at about half the price of a meal across the road in one of our restaurants.

Catering courses are now available all over the country, specializing in the various disciplines generally lumped together under the unlovely heading 'hospitality industry'. 'Catering', which I always think has a rather institutional ring to it, used to be something of a last resort for those whose qualifications were not quite up to scratch. Even as little as 15 years ago, many parents would have been disappointed if their children opted for such a career path. But whereas some young people might still see kitchen or restaurant work as simply better than nothing, others are more ambitious and motivated. Young people are attracted to the profession for a variety of reasons – they may have been encouraged to cook as children, their parents might be in the business themselves giving them some first-hand experience, they may be drawn to the theatre or creativity of the job or they simply may have seen celebrity chefs on television and fancied a go. Whatever the impulse, it is increasingly recognized that professional qualifications and passion are essential to make the grade.

Trainée waitresses in Morocco.

BIRGITTA ULMANDER

Head of the University of Orebrois Department of Restaurant and Culinary Arts, Grythyttan, Sweden

At Grythyttan we train not just chefs but waiters, managers and future restaurant owners. We approach the subject of food and restaurants in a holistic way, exploring and analysing what makes a good restaurant experience and how to make the customer happy. The course focuses on the various aspects of a restaurant visit and different elements of the meal. We have wonderful support from the industry and get many famous chefs, architects and restaurateurs coming as short-term lecturers.

We have identified various key variables that contribute to a good experience of eating out. If one of those factors is weak or missing, then the others have to be considerably better to compensate. We try and make our students think fast on their feet when things go wrong, in order to respond to difficult situations quickly and diplomatically.

Food and cooking are absolutely basic – what is on the customer's plate will always be vitally important. As well as classic and creative cuisine we teach nutrition and the food sciences, including various sensory approaches to food and drink. Restaurant design is also crucial, so we look at architecture, colour, fabrics, table settings, menu design and composition, as well as the quality and care of glassware, china and linen.

We believe the quality of a restaurant is apparent from the very first moment, as soon as someone enters a room or looks at a menu outside

or, even, from the way a telephone booking is handled. The first personal contact with the customer is crucial, so we teach the psychology of meeting and greeting and study body language. Some of our lecturers come from a theatrical background; running a restaurant is like a theatrical performance, with everyone working front-of-house playing a part.

For some restaurant goers, good food is not always the primary consideration; people may be looking for the right surroundings for a business meeting or a celebration, so we also study how to create a good atmosphere. Musicians and artists contribute to this aspect of the course because we believe other cultural dimensions can help us think in new ways.

Finally, we teach our students management systems and financial accounting, because you always have to be practical – and money, the balance sheet, is always there in the background.

Successful restaurants do indeed sometimes have an **X**-factor that is hard to define, but often when you sit down to analyse it you can find the answer. Last year some of our students studied two restaurants, one that was flourishing and one that was failing. The reason for the latter was simple to discover – the chef was in a bad mood all the time and there was a terrible atmosphere as a result! Very often the success of the restaurant comes down to just one person – owner or chef – and they've got to get it right.

Some excellent courses in catering and hotel management are available for the truly dedicated; French and Swiss catering schools are renowned. Cornell University in New York State offers a BSc degree in Hotel Administration and a Masters degree for post-graduates. The coursework covers organizational skills, food and beverage management, as well as marketing and finance. The school also runs a hotel – the Statler –which is used as a training ground for students; several of the courses at the school involve working positions at the hotel. Many major hotel and restaurant groups recruit heavily from Cornell; in fact, we made use of this resource when staffing our New York restaurants at Bridgemarket.

Our restaurants have extremely active personnel departments. Currently employing 1,200 people in 17 restaurants, we are one of the largest employers of chefs, porters, cleaners, managers, sommeliers, runners and waiters in London. We are also involved in a constant recruitment drive for replacement staff as well as for the new restaurants coming on line.

Personnel management in Britain is increasingly governed by a mass of bureaucracy, mostly coming from Brussels. The regulation with the biggest impact is the Working Time Directive. With 48 hours being the maximum allowed during a seven-day period, the practice of contracting by shifts will have to change. Until recently, a shift was anything between eight and 12 hours; the new directive will mean that shifts will have to be defined by hours, and breaks between and during shifts will have to be accounted for. Logging on and off will mean a massive increase in paperwork, a potential bureaucratic minefield. Other changes coming into force include mandatory medical checks for night-workers, compulsory ID checks to comply with the Asylum Act and a myriad of Health and Safety at Work regulations including a statutory 20 days of holiday for every employee.

For a new restaurant the key personnel who need to be recruited as a matter of priority are the general manager and the head chef. It is of paramount importance to have these positions filled as early in the project as economically possible. Both can offer a valuable input into the design, layout, systems and further recruitment for the restaurant. A chef will have useful ideas about the menu, how the kitchen should be designed, how much prep area will be required and how many chefs he will need in his brigade. The general manager will have views on which systems to install, the optimum layout of the restaurant and the front-of-house staffing numbers.

Finding these primary personnel is not always an easy job. The promotion policy in our restaurants is such that very often the company can move a manager, for example, from another one of our restaurants to the new enterprise, promoting someone from within the first restaurant to take his or her place. This is of three-fold benefit: promotion from within encourages loyalty among the staff, the new restaurant benefits from the experience gained in the other restaurant, which helps in the learning curve of any newly recruited staff, and the standards expected of the restaurant are more easily maintained. I do think it is important that promotions come from within and that there should be opportunities to move up from even the lowest rung on the ladder; the policy serves as a powerful incentive for the staff who have ability and show loyalty. A few years ago, the restaurant business was afflicted by a rash of job-jumping, as staff moved from restaurant to restaurant. Today, a long list of names on a CV is increasingly viewed by employers as evidence of a lack of commitment, rather than an impressive and varied career history.

Kingue Nkembe, manager at Bluebird, has been a beneficiary of this promotion policy, and so have we. A former law student, Kingue had had limited experience of hotel and catering work when he applied for a job at the not-yet-opened Quaglino's. His relative lack of experience meant that he joined the restaurant, not as a waiter, as he had hoped, but as a runner, tough, fast-paced work that involves racing backwards and forwards between dispatch in the kitchen and the waiter stations. Despite the intensity of the job, Kingue found that he loved the atmosphere and feeling of community. His manager noted his speed and his ambition and soon promoted Kingue to waiter, from which position he rose to become head waiter, acting as the conduit between waiters, runners, kitchen and management. Six years on from his days as a runner, he has now reached the position of manager, a role that makes the most of his skills with people, his analytical training and the experience he has gained first hand.

When there are several new restaurants opening within a short space of time, key staff may have to be recruited from outside and here the employment consultancies prove useful. The reputation of the employer can be a key factor in attracting good staff. It is easier to fill vacancies if you offer training, opportunities for career development, promotion from within the organization and decent pay. While large groups are better placed to provide such conditions, other applicants may well be drawn to the family atmosphere of a small restaurant which relies on the friendship and enthusiasm of the boss and the loyalty and cohesion of the staff, and that is why all our restaurants are run as individual entities.

Our restaurants frequently receive letters from hopeful would-be employees, looking for jobs as waiters, bar or kitchen staff. These are kept on file and, while the applicants may not get a job in the restaurant which they originally contacted, they may find an opportunity in another. Students, particularly those from France, Scandinavia and Italy, are very keen to gain work experience in London's restaurants. If you are intending to open a predominantly French restaurant, it is quite important to have at least a few French-speaking staff, likewise Italian staff for an Italian restaurant. When Michael Chow opened his upmarket Chinese restaurant in the late 1960s he caused quite a stir by staffing the restaurant with urbane Italian waiters, a policy which enhanced the sophisticated atmosphere and played an important part in the restaurant's success.

Restaurant roles

The traditional division of labour in the restaurant is between those who work in 'front-of-house' positions and those who work 'back-of-house', in other words, between waiting and cooking. In the old days, there was considerable animosity between the two camps. Waiters, with their starring role in the theatre of the restaurant, were often envied by the kitchen staff who toiled away behind the scenes. Such festering resentments no doubt accounted for the traditional restaurant cliché of the chef who spits in the soup. *Garçon*, a film made in the 1960s and starring Yves Montand, includes a wonderfully wicked scene where one of the sous chefs heats the side of a plate under the salamander or grill, whereupon the waiter, with whom he has an ongoing row, picks it up and burns his fingers.

In the past a chef cooked in his kitchen and that was it. The buying of produce was usually done by someone else. The chef was isolated from the rest of the world, from his suppliers and, most importantly, from his customers. Today, all this has changed. The chef's job encompasses varied and demanding responsibilities, and the rewards, both in terms of payment and job satisfaction, are also greater. The Butlers Wharf Chef School has seen a number of young men and women leaving good jobs in the City and successfully training to be chefs.

With the increase in the number of smaller restaurants, owned and managed by those passionate about food, have come chefs who share the same approach. They care about their ingredients, are creative with their menus and are increasingly knowledgeable about suppliers. Contemporary chefs also have to be managers, training staff and running their team to get the best results.

As many chefs have told me, one of the contributory factors in this shift of attitude is the visibility of the kitchen from the restaurant. Breaking down the barriers has ended the chef's solitary confinement in a greasy basement or backroom. When chefs can see the pleasure of customers as they eat the food they have created and share in the general atmosphere, their sense of responsibility and pride is enhanced. Kitchen visibility means kitchens have to be far more presentable, which in turn means better working conditions – and if anyone spits in the soup, they're in full view. In fact, chefs have become so visible these days that it can be difficult to persuade them to stay in the kitchen. Celebrity chefs, promoting products, judging competitions, taking part in panel games, starring in their own television programmes and selling books, have become the media flavour of the month. While it is excellent to see chefs gain public recognition, there is a danger that all the attention diverts them from their real job: cooking.

Perhaps in reaction to the type of restaurant whose reputation rests more or less entirely on the star quality of its chef has come another shift in attitude, with the front-of-house virtues of discreet, adroit management and service increasingly to the fore. Historically, the British have not been

In a large restaurant kitchen, everyone has a specific role.

renowned for their waiting skills. Whereas Italians embraced the idea of waiting with relish and style, and the French with professionalism and competence, the British have tended to view the job as a dead-end and acted accordingly. I sympathize with those who find the boot-camp school of waiting unacceptable. There is no longer anything smart or eccentric about rude waiters – and probably never was, although I do know of one or two restaurants who enjoyed their staffs' reputation for bad behaviour.

As with kitchen work, improvements in conditions, better pay and prospects for promotion mean that waiting is now seen as a job to be taken seriously, one of the first steps on the ladder to management. This has made a difference, too, in the customer's attitude – waiters are more likely to be treated with respect, thus making their job a considerably more pleasant one. The waiter is the focus of contact between the kitchen and the customer and to a great extent he or

she, together with other members of the front-of-house team, are every bit as responsible for the diner's enjoyment as the food itself. I believe that the 'optional service charge' is a good system for encouraging the waiter to take care of the customer. If a tip is withheld by a customer because the service was poor, the restaurant management can investigate and take steps to rectify the situation. This serves to keep the staff on their toes.

A good waiter will achieve the proper balance of attention and discretion. There are few things as irritating as an overly zealous waiter, one who constantly hovers, filling the glasses with a millimetre of wine after every sip, fussing with the place settings, adjusting the salt and pepper, always on the brink of interruption. On the other hand, a waiter who appears to be looking in every direction but yours is equally frustrating, although perhaps not as infuriating as one who is most interested in chatting to his colleagues.

Waiters should be fully briefed on each dish so that they can help the customers choose suitably and engage in a little meaningful dialogue. Never be tempted to instruct your staff to itemize the components of every dish fully; it wastes time and is vastly irritating. There is an incredibly popular restaurant in London, with something like a five-week waiting list for tables on Friday evenings, where the maître d', in an accent of Pythonesque hilarity, recounts in minute detail the content, technique and the presentation of every dish to his customers. I visited this restaurant, found the food impeccable, but will not return because the obsequiousness of this delivery ruins the evening.

Restaurant management is another fine art. A good chef is an obvious asset, but a good manager is equally crucial. Discretion, charm and stamina, coupled with skills in staff management and budget control, an eye for detail, a ready shoulder to cry on, a willingness to muck-in and tactful handling of difficult customers are all necessary qualities. Depending on the restaurant and the individuals, we employ floor managers, restaurant managers and general managers, in ascending order of responsibility. Part of these managerial positions involves adminstration and the smooth operation of a team of people. On a daily basis, the restaurant manager needs to ensure all his or her staff are organized and ready to run their respective sections of the restaurant. He or she coordinates the action between the kitchen, bar and front-of-house, making sure that everyone has the necessary information regarding daily specials and what dishes are off the menu, that the drinks are in place, the wines have arrived, the restaurant is clean, the flowers are fresh and everything is as it should be.

Once the service is underway, the manager's role is to keep things moving. Which table is ready for the main course? Who is content to stay

In the film *Garçon*, the tension between the kitchen and the front-of-house staff results in increasing farce – great for a movie, but not for a restaurant.

GEORGE LANG

Co-owner of Café des Artistes, New York, and Gundel and The Owl's Castle, Budapest, author of *The Cuisine of Hungary* and *No One Knows the Truffles I've Seen*

The reason why motivating staff is so important is simple and obvious – a happy staff makes happy guests. You must really, truly and without reservation, respect and care about your employees. Perhaps once a year a chef or manager can afford the luxury of acting like the king of the jungle, but a constant reign of terror is counterproductive – eventually it simply won't register at all or it may result in retaliation where the service or produce is sabotaged.

At our Budapest restaurants we throw the best party of the year for the kids of our employees, complete with desserts, hot chocolate, clowns, magicians and bags of goodies. You have to keep the ideas flowing. Try introducing competitions, such as one based on selling the most wine on a monthly basis. Promote from within if possible, instead of going to an employment agency or trying to steal someone from another restaurant. Money, of course, is a fairly reliable motivator. At our Budapest operations we have implemented a profit-sharing plan. Bear in mind, though, that to come up with the right plan you have to have the heart of a loving mother, the head of a financial expert and the experience of a professional restaurateur. For instance, some chefs may try to lower their food costs to achieve the required figures for the profit-sharing plan by cutting corners on quality of meat, portion sizes and so on.

When we hire a new waiter, he or she is first assigned to a seasoned waiter so they can trail them for several weeks. At the same time, they must memorize our bible, The Rules of Service, that describes everything from a proper table set-up to the way to hold the bottle when pouring wine. The Rules of Service lists each dish on the menu with instructions regarding its ingredients and cooking method, where to pick it up, what utensils must be on the table before serving it, also the questions the guests might ask – all organized in a neat, easy-to-read horizontal grid system. I am convinced that using this simple but vital system would reduce the dismaying percentage of restaurant failures.

It is so important to make the customer feel special, to make them leave happy and return again. Greet guests warmly – with their names, if possible – and make them feel as though they are invited to the dining room of a family. If the farewell is also the kind you would offer a friend leaving your house, it might even compensate for a less-than-perfect meal.

To be a successful restaurateur is something that can be taught or cultivated and many professionals deliver workmanlike, respectable performances. However, to become a great restaurateur demands a certain spark which carries something that is beyond learning, a magical seasoning of passion and enthusiasm.

in the bar for another drink; who needs to be seated immediately? Has the guest arrived who will be joining the customer already at the table? Keen powers of observation are essential to oversee the complex choreography of service, together with nerves of steel.

An equally important part of the manager's role is to act as the 'face of the restaurant', meeting and greeting customers, recognizing regulars and accommodating their particular needs and generally adding personality to the professionalism of the staff. In this respect the restaurant manager acts as a traditional maître d'hotel, a role of some subtlety and skill. As evidenced in the story by Ludwig Bemelmans to which I referred in the first section, the true hallmark of a good maître d' is 'anticipation', meaning that sixth sense that prevents things from going horribly wrong. An excellent memory for faces and superior people skills are invaluable. A high calibre maître d' will know the restaurant's regulars and will take care to seat his customers to avoid the type of embarassing situations that can unexpectedly occur when business rivals occupy adjoining tables or both

halves of a divorced couple arrive at the restaurant on the same night with their new partners. As with so much else involved in the front-of-house operations, when the job is done well, you can barely tell that it has been done at all.

Working in a restaurant is demanding at the best of times, but occasionally something quite unexpected happens which really puts staff to the test. One day an elderly lady who was dining at the Bluebird Club choked on her beef and very nearly died. A quick-thinking waiter administered emergency first aid; another member of staff organized an ambulance to take the lady to hospital. The staff then followed up the unfortunate incident by sending flowers. A few days later, they received a letter from the woman's husband, expressing his gratitude for their swift action, which he was certain had saved his wife's life. He was also most anxious to reassure them that the beef had not been tough!

The buzz

There is something truly wonderful about a kitchen in full swing – the chef presiding over his brigade, dishes coming over the pass on to the waiters' trays and being whisked out into the dining room. Flames leaping from the grill, the sudden clouds of steam as lids are lifted off huge bubbling pans, the tight choreography of teamwork all add to the theatrical spectacle.

This theatricality attracts people to work in the business. Ask anyone from a bus boy to the managing director of a large restaurant group why they chose to work in a restaurant, their answers always involve words such as 'people', 'atmosphere', 'challenge' and 'the buzz'. Some newcomers realize soon that the business is not for them – the long, unsocial hours and hard, physically demanding work does result in a significant drop-out rate – but many others are quickly bitten by the bug and fall in love with the whole way of life.

Against all the odds, and despite the frantic pace, restaurants have a special quality for those who work in them. Every service is like a theatrical performance, with the menu as the script, and the waiters and chefs as the cast. Staff perform flat out, wind down, and then it all starts again with a new audience.

Every member of staff has their own challenge. For the chef it's the chance to put his skill to the test, his art on a plate, whether it is 50 plates a day or 2,500. For the manager it's the challenge of keeping customers as happy and contented as his staff, for the sommelier it may just be the opportunity to sell a rare vintage or to select the perfect accompaniment to a meal. The porter may have ambitions to become a chef – several of our chefs de partie started their careers as a 'boy in blue'. A waiter may be doing the job between parts, but it's more likely that he's doing it for the job satisfaction, the pay and share of the 'tronc' – the tips, the atmosphere and the interaction with the customers. But everyone is in it for the buzz. When I recently asked a commis chef why he worked in the hell-for-leather kitchen at Bluebird his reply – "Top fun" – enchanted me.

There's an increasing sense of expectation as a restaurant gears up for service. Here, at Mash in London, waiters check to see that all the tables are properly laid up.

A day in the life of a chef

David Burke has been chef director at Le Pont de la Tour since it opened in 1991. He was previously at Bibendum and, before that, at Ballymaloe in County Cork. David spends about four hours a week actually cooking; the rest of his time is devoted to administration, ordering supplies, staff meetings and checking the quality of the food prepared by his brigade. Despite the fact that he is ultimately responsible for 100 jobs in the restaurant and kitchen, David is perfectly prepared to roll up his sleeves and do some hands-on maintenance if necessary. This willingness is indicated by the contents of his knife roll, which includes, as well as knives and a sharpener, a pair of pliers, a calculator, a phase tester and cross-head screwdrivers.

Monday morning, 7am: Every week has a new menu, and David Burke is going through this week's with his head chef, Earl Cameron. The menu at Pont makes the most of seasonal foods – early spring sees lamb, asparagus, Cornish crab and wild Scottish salmon; autumn menus are strong on game, fungi and winter root vegetables.

Monday is a busy day for deliveries as a steady stream of fresh produce floods through the back doors. The huge crates of sole, turbot and langoustines – all of which are creel-caught, packed in ice and then flown down live from Scotland – are taken straight into the kitchen for preparation. The freshest asparagus and salad leaves are rushed in, as are racks of lamb from Devon and aged sides of beef. During the summer months, David uses my Berkshire garden as the source for his herbs and soft seasonal

fruits, and this is on top of the wonderful range of vegetables which are grown specially for the restaurant.

The quality of the food is imperative to a successful restaurant, so as produce is delivered, it is weighed and checked, then despatched to the prep area or cold store. Even though David has built up relationships with his suppliers over the years, sometimes the food is not up to scratch. A delivery of sole is rejected for being too small and the French beans that were ordered are not available; the alternative is mange-tout or peas. Considering this week's menu, the peas are the best choice.

At 9am the kitchen is already bustling with chefs preparing the day's lunch. David is on the phone placing orders for the rest of the week before dashing across the kitchen to fillet the great side of a Greek blue-fin tuna. Elsewhere a stockpot is simmering, the pâtissier is burnishing the tops of lemon custard tarts with a blow torch, the sauce chef is preparing racks of lamb for a lunch in the salon privé and all the while one of the porters is sweeping and mopping the floor, removing the constant flow of food preparation rubbish.

At 11am there's a chance to get out of the ever-increasing temperature of the kitchen for a 10-minute breakfast break. David then has the chance to brief the restaurant staff about the new menu and answer any questions that may arise. It is of the utmost importance that they know the dishes and can talk about them to the customer with confidence. Now's the time for the final checks before the lunch service: is the soup ready? Are all the fish prepared? And are the chefs ready for yet another manic lunchtime service? David goes and changes into his chef's whites.

Lunchtime in the kitchen becomes a complex ballet, all cleverly choreographed by David. Orders are called and the chefs begin work. Hot and cold dishes, ready simultaneously, are picked up by the runners and rushed to the waiter stations and thence to the customers. There's a constant chorus of chefs shouting to one another with a background noise of plates, glasses, knives and forks being scraped and stacked.

By 3pm the orders are starting to thin. Ideally this would be a time to relax, but there's the evening to prepare for, so already fish are being scaled, veal sliced, chickens trussed and vegetables peeled. By 3.50pm only one table remains occupied. David and his head chef give a critique of the lunch service, establish who will be on duty for the evening and return to the office to tackle the mountain of paperwork, return all the phone calls and deal with any other issues that may have arisen during the day. There's just time for a quick cigarette and a cup of coffee before it's back to the kitchen and into the fray of the evening service.

Chairman and Yip, Canberra

Sartoria, London

Balthazar, New York

Jean-Georges, New York

It's nothing in comparison to the demands of a busy service, but there's lots of preparation to be done before the first customer arrives: the chef and restaurant manager may need to discuss changes to the menu, and staff in the kitchen and front-of-house have to be briefed. As chefs begin their prep, so waiters start to clean and lay up the restaurant.

Blue Print Café, London

Kitchen at Paul Bocuse, Lyon

Kitchen at Pierre Gagnaire, Paris

Kitchen in Shanghai

Kitchen at Mezzo, London

Restaurant kitchens may consist of a single chef or a team numbering several dozen. It's essential that everyone knows what they have to do and, particularly in a big kitchen, that everything runs smoothly so that all the food reaches the restaurant pass at the same time. At Paul Bocuse's kitchen in Lyon, Michelin standards cannot be allowed to slip, and activity in the kitchen is fantastically labour-intensive; in a Shanghai kitchen, by contrast, the greatest imperative is to feed the customers as quickly and efficiently as possible.

Briefing chefs at Coq d'Argent, London

Wagamama, London

The best number for a dinner party is two – **myself** *and* **a dam' good head waiter**

NUBAR GULBENKIAN

Quaglino's, London

Good service can make all the difference between a good meal and a wonderful one... but getting the level of attention right can be tricky. We all have different expectations according to the type of mood we're in, the reason for going out for a meal, the other people we are with, whether or not we have been to the restaurant before. Factors such as the customer's age and where he or she lives can also play a part. Of course, different types of restaurants also bring with them different expectations of service: generally speaking, the more expensive the meal, the greater the level of attention. But whether you have dropped in to a noodle bar or are splashing out on a five-course banquet, it helps to be able to recognize staff. Uniforms can be as casual as a T-shirt or as formal as a frock-coat.

Re-creation of waiter's uniform (c. 1900), Delmonico's, New York

Imperial Banquet, Beijing

La Contea, Piemount, near Turin

Whilst there are restaurants that have built legendary reputations on the rudeness of their staff, this is generally a recipe for disaster.
A warm welcome and familiarity with the menu are always good signs of confident and competent waiters.

Ajit Bawan Hotel, Rajasthan, Jodhpur

Orrery, London

Ajit Bawan Hotel, Rajasthan, Jodhpur

Orrery, London

Occasionally you get that little bit extra from restaurant staff – such as the maître d' who really knows how to work a room, the passionate sommelier . . . or alternatively, in the right place at the right time, the flirtatious drag queen lighting your cigar.

Transvestite cigarette seller, Alcazar, Paris

Head sommelier, Paul Bocuse, Lyon

Tapas bar, Andalucia

Le Bistrot de Lyon, Lyon

Hostaria Farnese, Rome

Ratners, New York

Fats, London

Casual service should not be a by-word for shoddy or slapdash: you can almost feel the pride of the waiters at the tapas counter, the guy in the New York diner or the care with which a young waiter opens an oyster.

Caffè Toscanini, Amsterdam

At the end of a long day, when the last customers have gone, there's still more work to do. In really big restaurants, a typical working day can run almost the full 24 hours. And no matter how small your restaurant, there is cashing-up and accounts, washing-up and laundry to be done. But the end of service can also be a chance to put your feet up with a glass of wine, talk over any problems that arose during the service and plan for another day. The long and demanding hours of restaurant life mean that colleagues can become like an extended family.

Caffè Toscanini, Amsterdam

Le Pasteur, Lyon

detail

For me, one of the pleasures of running your own business is that you can address every detail, down to the typeface on the menus and the quality of the napkins.

Perhaps I am a control-freak, but **I cannot help taking great pleasure in being able to work on just about every detail** when we are planning a restaurant. Working with teams of in-house designers, we look at every aspect of how a restaurant will be presented, **from the upholstery of the chairs to the uniforms of the waiters,** from commissioning a piece of art to designing the ashtray.

Some people claim this is tantamount to opening a theme restaurant, but I would have to disagree. Burger bars stuffed with memorabilia aim to create an experience in which the food has a minor role; the trick of such businesses is to encourage customers to 'upspend', as they say, on T-shirts and souvenirs. By contrast, **our own restaurants look to take their cue from the heritage of the building or the location:** so, for example, Sartoria, on Savile Row, uses tailoring as one of its points of reference, but I would never want such motifs to overwhelm the restaurant or, worse, the food that is coming out of the kitchen. **Detail is an opportunity to have some fun** and attention to detail is a good indication that a place is truly cared for.

Detail is never insignificant, especially when it comes to restaurants. To some extent the customer is a captive audience, with time to notice the finer points of presentation and an expectation, until proved otherwise, that everything will be perfect. This sense of expectation is, however, quite fragile and can be quickly overturned by what might seem minor inconveniences or shortfalls. The right details may not be immediately apparent, but they carry on working at an almost subconscious level to perpetuate a happy mood of contentment and anticipation. The wrong details, by contrast, strike an all too obvious jarring note and undermine whatever enjoyment may be gained from the food itself.

'Detail' is perhaps too focused a word for what can encompass quite significant elements of design and conception. Considered in the context of restaurants, detail is the flavour or identity of a place, worked out through a myriad small decisions concerning everything from the typeface on the menu and the flowers at the entrance to the signs on the lavatory doors. If the spatial design and menu provide the operational outline for the restaurant, detail is the paintbox that colours it.

Working out these finer points is my favourite part of every new project. When all the decisions on location and on financing have been made, the architects have drawn up their plans for the basic shell and we are convinced that the space will work, I retreat somewhere quiet, armed with a huge supply of layout pads and 3B pencils to begin the process of imagining the restaurant into life. Fixtures and fittings, flooring, furniture, graphics, table settings, staff uniforms – every single detail down to the restaurant name contributes to its identity and character.

In Mezzo, many of the finishing touches take their lead from the colours used by Allan Jones in the mural he painted for the restaurant.

There's a fine line between paying careful attention to detail and over-designing a space. A slick interior scheme, impeccable furniture and sumptuous flowers can be wonderful in themselves, but the end result can be bland and lacking in vitality if there is nothing personal, quirky or idiosyncratic to take some of the edge off the glacial perfection. In such sublime surroundings, the customer is almost an intruder and only those who are either exceptionally confident or stupendously oblivious will feel at ease there. Another type of over-design is the pretentious variety, where a fussy, elaborate scheme in which everything down to the menu is decorated, trimmed and embellished is the restaurant equivalent of keeping up with the Joneses.

The design scheme

The starting point for the design scheme is to conjure up a specific mood or atmosphere from memories of past pleasures, creating a character that reflects both the location and architectural qualities of the space. At Le Pont de la Tour, the long, low lines of the space and its riverside setting suggested the glamour of a 1940s' piano bar crossed with elements of a cruise liner – vaguely retro and classically chic. At Mezzo, it was the history of the site as a noted music venue which inspired the clean, jazzy, contemporary style used there; the design ideas for Sartoria, located in the heart of London's bespoke tailoring district, came about as an oblique reference to its location and were distilled from my memories of austere restaurants I visited in Italy in the early 1950s. Translating such musings into a scheme for fitting-out and furnishing is the next stage in the process.

Cocktail stirrers, drinks mats and condiments all provide opportunities to reinforce the identity of a restaurant.

The type of furniture, fittings, flooring and materials chosen for a restaurant is the way to turn preliminary ideas into reality. These may seem to be no more than aesthetic choices, but the management and maintenance of a restaurant is far more successful in the long run if such issues are addressed in the early stages of the project. Detail is all about definition and a defining image or character can provide an important sense of coherence for the staff as much as a strong identity for the customer.

Here it is important to distinguish between a restaurant with a strong sense of identity and one which is 'themed'. The line between the two is undoubtedly a fine one to tread, but I think the principal difference is that the themed restaurant or bar has a certain relentless quality, rather like a joke whose punchline gets repeated too often. It's ultimately a question of balance. The identity of a restaurant should reveal itself in the smaller details, not overwhelm the spatial qualities of the site or the flavour of the location.

As far as fitting-out and furnishing the restaurant are concerned, it is important to invest in good, natural materials that will last well, that need less frequent replacement and have the potential to improve with a little wear and tear. The same is true of the basic design concept. Up-to-the-minute design may draw in the fashion conscious in droves in the first few months but will date very quickly: what is cutting edge today is bound to need replacing two years hence, much to the dismay of the restaurateur or the restaurant's financial backers. Restaurants which use their inherited features with sensitivity and intelligence will still look good in years to come. A patina of careful use and appreciative patronage is very attractive.

The type of restaurant that you are planning will also affect your approach to the design scheme. At the upper end of the market, a luxurious style can be conveyed with low, romantic and glamorous lighting, maybe supplemented by candles or shaded lamps on the tables. Generosity is also important – larger tables set further apart, large plates, side plates and good quality glasses. Tables should be dressed with tablecloths and flowers. Quiet, soft and pale colours reinforce the message – and are all the more expensive to keep clean.

In less expensive restaurants, where a much faster turnover is expected, lighting will generally be brighter and less subtle. The surfaces in such a venue will generally be hard-wearing and durable, and probably in strong colours that are also easy to clean. Very often there is no facility to make reservations and customers are happy to take the chance, turn up and sit at long refectory-style tables. Casual restaurants tend not to have tablecloths and linen napkins, though here I draw the line: we have cotton damask napkins in all our restaurants even though they cost something like nine pence a time to launder.

In terms of detail, the bottom line for customers is often physical comfort. The right level of lighting, enough space between tables to avoid claustrophobia or the unpleasant suspicion that the next table is eavesdropping on your private conversation, chairs and banquettes that are the right height and tables that don't wobble will not guarantee a perfect lunch or an evening to remember, but they are no less essential in terms of basic enjoyment.

The choice of chair for a restaurant, for example, conveys a distinct message. Quick service, fast turnover, busy, bustling and noisy places are often defined by the use of hard, upright and easily movable and stackable chairs. The classic Thonet bentwood chairs are ideal for the purpose; unlike many simple chairs, their springy resilience ensures that they are both comfortable and supportive. Furthermore, they rarely break and have been a consistent feature of cafés, bistros and brasseries for over a century. The modern interpretation of these classics is the chair I chose for Quaglino's, Mezzonine and Alcazar. Originally designed for use in the US Navy and high-security American prisons, the chair is light, strong, virtually unbreakable and, despite its origins, far from a punishment to sit in.

For more leisurely dining and to put across an impression of luxury, chairs should be upholstered. While the Bar and Grill at Le Pont de la Tour has durable upright chairs, the restaurant is furnished with armchairs with large padded seats. The enveloping chairs at Bibendum, with their slipcovers that change with the seasons, are almost too comfortable – some diners have been reluctant to leave them until the small hours. The ultimate, however, are the little sofas in Sartoria, which are divinely comfortable.

Aside from the comfort they offer, well-upholstered chairs are excellent sound absorbers, in the same way as tablecloths, rugs and fabric wallcoverings. At Mezzo we employed two different strategies with respect to sound. For Mezzonine, on the upper level, we wanted to encourage the buzzy, loud Soho atmosphere, so we used the same chairs as Quaglino's. Downstairs, in the more upmarket Mezzo restaurant we have used an upholstered seat with a hard back: with live jazz in the evening, we did not want the restaurant to have too many sound-absorbing elements.

Graphics

The importance of a strong graphic identity cannot be over-emphasized. A memorable graphic identity perpetuates the integrity of the overall design concept of a restaurant; a weak image makes the whole enterprise look untidy and directionless. It's not simply a question of designing the sign over the door, the type on the menu or the box of matches: good graphic design can trigger an association with a good experience, an enjoyable evening, a memorable meal. You merely have to consider the graphics of brands such as Chanel, Gucci, Coca-Cola or even McDonalds to see that a strong image says more than a lengthy description ever could. We take great care to carry the graphic design to the back-of-house areas. It is important that the staff get the signal that every little detail really matters.

When we acquired the premises for Quaglino's we also wanted to take over that historic and memorable name. After a few exchanges of letters and not a little nail biting, we secured it. We needed a strong image that was new and modern without losing the glamour that the name invoked. After playing around with a few options I came up with the idea of using the initial Q. This strong calligraphic image now forms the basis of all the restaurant's graphics.

The next step was to draw up a list of items that could possibly carry the image: printed material, interior and exterior signage, ashtrays, plates, glasses, wine labels and even the buttons of the uniforms. In itself, the printed material encompasses a huge range of items – the menus and wine lists, the bills and bill holders, matches, bar coasters and all the promotional literature. The Q has also been incorporated into elements of the interior design, including the balustrade of the main staircase and the etched glass screens on the central banquette. So successful has the Q been, the ashtray

The Quaglino's 'Q' provides a graphic that runs through the restaurant, from the sweeping staircase banister to the memorable (and much-stolen!) ashtrays.

has become something of a trophy for many of our diners and the rate of loss is in the region of 800 per month! The apparent desirability of such items prompted us to open a small shop within Quaglino's selling (apart from the ashtrays) glasses, small leather goods, cufflinks, tie-pins, cigarette lighters and other accessories, as well as our own wine and champagne.

The Zinc Bar & Grill, a completely different concept, had different demands. At Zinc, the service is less attentive – the food arrives at the table already 'plated' and you pour your own wine. There is a rack of newspapers, posters of local art events, no dress policy and a proportion of tables left for diners who may turn up without booking. To go with the casual atmosphere, we wanted an image that was simple, with the ability to be applied to a limited range of items, but with a broad appeal. The colour palette of the graphic identity we devised has been applied in the decorative scheme, as well as serving to differentiate the wine labels, menus and other printed material. Echoing the simplicity in the cooking and presentation of the food, the menu appears to be manually typed, is printed on inexpensive paper and is left on the table.

Sartoria provided an opportunity for subtle, quirky humour – combining images derived from the tailoring tradition of Savile Row with those suggesting Italian cooking. The wit of Sartoria's graphics – tailor's shears snipping a piece of lasagne, a porcini pin cushion, a needle threaded with spaghetti, salami being measured with a tailor's rule and ravioli being cut with pinking shears – help to temper the rather formal and austere nature of the interior design.

Although I view graphic design as part of the overall concept of the restaurant, many of the menus that I have found most memorable are those that have not actually been designed by a designer. A good example is the typical purple-ink jelly-pad menu found in French bistros. Printed every day, the dishes reflecting what was available in the market that morning, the faint aroma of methylated spirit coming from the paper is an aperitif in itself, while the uniformity of the French hand, with its loops and flourishes, is both distinctive and readable. In a slightly more sophisticated vein, Brasserie Lipp in Paris has a marvellously clear, simple menu, with red ink used to highlight dishes that are special or good value. Marco Pierre White was inspired by the menu at Taillevent; his menu at Mirabelle faithfully reproduces the style down to a crossed T. David Hockney's menus designed for Langan's Brasserie, Odins and Neal Street are still in use and look every bit as good as they did in the 1970s.

How much investment should a first-time restaurateur put into the graphic design of the menu? For a small restaurant, particularly if you are just starting out, a blackboard listing all the dishes can be perfectly adequate, but a really good hand is mandatory and one must keep the dictat 'less is more' firmly in mind and avoid squiggles and flourishes, Technicolor chalk, a typographer's sampler of styles and any other embellishment that makes the menu hard to read. When I opened The Soup Kitchen, I was inspired by Jules Gouffé's great gastro bible *Livre de Cuisine* when it came to creating a graphic identity. I used the steel engravings and plain roman typeface that he featured for the decoration and signage of the restaurant but relied on a blackboard to show which soups were available that day.

Writing the menu presents its own challenges. Where do you pitch the language? While it may once have been amusing to read those flowery, romantic novellas of menus – everything 'hand-gathered at dawn' or 'resting in a limpid pool of seductive sauce' – that sort of description does pall rather quickly. Many restaurants adopt an equally irritating hybrid French-English gastro-language, which is further complicated by the introduction of techniques and ingredients from the Far East, India, Japan, North Africa and the Americas.

Simplicity is best. State the main ingredient, and whether it's grilled, poached, braised or roasted, and mention the accompanying sauce. It is not necessary to itemize the bunch of watercress or sprig of chervil used for garnish. Many restaurant dishes today incorporate ingredients with which their customers are not always familiar, but instead of getting into lengthy descriptions on the menu itself, it is much better to let the customer ask the waiter. An informed dialogue between customer and waiter is of importance in a good restaurant.

Uniforms

Surprisingly, uniforms also play a significant role in the design concept of a restaurant. They maintain the design integrity of the whole and define the hierarchy of the staff within the restaurant, which is important for both customers and employees.

When we were designing Quaglino's, we felt that the glamour of the space called for really special uniforms. Showing a strong streak of nepotism, I asked my son Jasper, who has enormous experience in tailoring, couture and theatrical costume design, to come up with a scheme. With about 100 staff working on each shift, creating uniforms for everyone was something of a challenge. Managers, head waiters, waiters, runners, barmen, chefs, porters, doormen, lavatory attendants, receptionists and the cigarette girl all had to be clothed.

The uniform for the managers and head waiters are plain black suits. In the beginning, the suits were made in traditional medium weight wool suiting, but very soon we discovered that wear and tear, together with the frequent dry-cleaning that was necessary, meant that the suits wore out very quickly. Six weeks was the average before the suits fell to pieces – the greeters literally had holes in their trousers from running up and down the stairs a couple of hundred times a shift. In the light of this, it was necessary to find an alternative fabric, which would provide more durability but would also have a good appearance and be comfortable for the staff to wear. We discovered that there were some extraordinarily durable fabrics available but most of these materials had a school uniform look about them. In the end, we decided upon a heavy-duty wool, which was expensive but well worth the investment in the long term.

The uniforms for the waiters and runners were simple Nehru-collared jackets – striped for the waiters and plain blue for the runners. The barmen are in white and the crustacea chefs sport crew-necked striped jerseys in a style that is reminiscent of Breton fishermen. We found that the same type of uniforms lent themselves to being adapted in Mezzo and Mezzonine. The blue and green waiters' and runners' jackets add an effective splash of colour to the kitchen when customers see the staff lining up to collect the orders. By contrast, the casual atmosphere of Zinc is defined by the open-necked shirts or T-shirts and aprons of the waiters.

Equipment

Because we have designed and equipped so many restaurants we have been able to put together a restaurant designer's and manager's bible, known as the Purchasing Manual. The manual was collated by our buying department based on the experience gained from every restaurant opening. It lists every possible item that a restaurant might need: the obvious things like plates and glasses, cups and saucers, knives and forks as well as the less obvious – toothpicks, candles, fire extinguishers, disposable gloves, coffee machines, stationery and till rolls. There are about 500 items in all, everything you can think of and many you would never imagine. The comprehensiveness of the list enables us to decide which items are needed in a particular restaurant, and whether we need to put the name or logo on that product, or indeed if we need to find or design something new. Even a small new restaurant requires a huge number of different things to operated efficiently and successfully.

The new projects department of Conran restaurants has responsibility for maintaining these 'non-food supplies' and setting up a catalogue database. The manager of the restaurant interacts with the development team and the Conran designers. The manager is responsible, too, for the presentation and buying of tableware, uniforms, cookware and cutlery for each new restaurant.

It would be easy if we could to use the same table-top paraphernalia in every case, but one of the more attractive aspects of our restaurants is that they each have a very individual look and feel. We have a 'collection' of restaurants rather than a group or chain. Each one is designed and crafted for its particular location, price range and menu. Part of the challenge – and the pleasure – of the job is ensuring that each restaurant is distinct.

Restaurant graphics, tableware and cutlery all give clues to the type of restaurant the owners hope to create: most people, whether or not they have heard of New York's Jean-Georges, would have high expectations of a restaurant that pays such subtle attention to detail.

We do, however, have an enormous advantage when it comes to the sourcing of table-top items – the Conran team of designers and buyers. Our restaurants can take full advantage of their skills and include products sourced or designed for the shops in the range of restaurant ware. Nevertheless, products that are designed for a predominately domestic market sometimes have to be tweaked in production for the hard life they will encounter in a restaurant. We find that handles have to be triple-welded and silverplate-ware needs to be 15 microns thick as opposed to ten for domestic ware. The dishwasher in a restaurant makes a carwash look like a hand-held shower and china needs to be robust enough to withstand the endless washing and dense enough to hold heat. Glasses chip less if they have a melted edge.

Knives, forks and spoons, too, have to stand up to heavy-duty dishwashing. When we were equipping Quaglino's, the first of our really large restaurants at some 300 covers, the manager suggested that it might be a good idea to use the same knife and fork for every savoury course, and the same spoon for soups and puddings. We designed a set accordingly. This uncomplicated and informal use of cutlery has subsequently been used with great success in many of our restaurants.

The restaurant manager has a useful input at the set-up stage too, advising on the number of glasses needed for wines, long and short drinks, water, liqueurs; jugs for water and Pimms; salt and pepper sets, lobster claw crackers, finger bowls and wine buckets. All such items have a place and a purpose, which means planning their storage and training the staff in their handling and maintenance.

Sometimes, something a little special is called for. A memorable feature of Coq d'Argent is the shallow silver sauté pans in which the food is cooked and brought to the table, still sizzling. I have always been charmed by such dishes – they were one of George Perry Smith's trademarks in the early days of The Hole in the Wall in Bath – and I managed to have some similar pans made for use in Coq d'Argent.

Focal points

At Quaglino's, the mosaic crustacea 'altar' at the end of the room, the theatrical sweep of the staircase and the eight columns, each painted by a different artist, define different areas within the space and add to the glamour of the interior. Mezzonine's rather austere interior is relieved by the marvellous photographic reportage of Soho life by Helen Drew. The

DNA, the bar above Quo Vadis restaurant in Soho, created quite a stir when it opened by acquiring work by Damien Hirst and other YBA's, shown here. When Marco Pierre White subsequently fell out with Hirst, he replaced the art with some of his own paintings!

COLMAN ANDREWS
Editor of *Saveur*

SAVEUR

Savor a World of Authentic Cuisine

PARIS RESTAURANT SECRETS

ARGENTINA: *Where the World's Best Beef Is Just the Beginning*
The Tang of SORREL AND GOOSEBERRIES · *Very Cool* ICE CREAM
ITALIAN FARMHOUSE *Cooking* · COBB SALAD *the Right Way*

35

" I have spent a significant part of my adult life eating in restaurants. My work gives me an excellent opportunity to discover, observe and sample, criticize or celebrate a vast variety of restaurants all over the world.

While I believe that design plays a subservient role to food in restaurants, I would not go so far as to say that the food is the single most important thing. What counts is the 'whole', not any one of the parts. I can certainly count among my favourite restaurants places where the food is not of exalted quality. Similarly, there are innumerable good and successful restaurants in various parts of the world which are 'undesigned', or which have been decorated rather than designed. And I think it's pretty clear to anyone who has any experience of the two-and three-star restaurants of France, that the *Guide Michelin* does not rate places according to the visual sophistication of the surroundings.

I've had excellent meals in bustling restaurants in various cities where the decor consisted of grease-coated Formica and synthetic wood panelling, ditto in unpretentious family restaurants which offer home cooking in a warm, thoroughly non-touristic settings. A shack on a beach, a cantina in the back of a garage, a lean-to on the side of the street in Denpasar – lots of great food in places where design doesn't feature in the owner's vocabulary.

Where restaurants are increasingly seen as 'events', particularly in certain capitals, stimulating design is probably pretty much an essential. I'm old fashioned enough to believe, however, that restaurants should always offer a modicum of comfort to diners – whatever else they do!

Themed restaurants seem to have been born here in America. To me they always seem somewhat calculated – something to do with marketing surveys and ten-year plans and focus groups. They certainly have their place in the industry, but in my experience they are generally not very interesting, chiefly because they fail to express any passion. Much more attractive is the current trend towards stripped-down but high-quality design and food.

Whatever a restaurant looks like, it certainly should give its customers what they want at prices they deem affordable, and it should deliver the goods consistently. Even more than a smart designer, a good chef or a topnotch maître d'hotel, what makes a restaurant successful is a restaurateur with vision, passion, and both the willingness and the ability to pay attention to every detail. That and good fried potatoes. "

idiosyncratic metre-high cockerel that dominates the entrance to Coq d'Argent is the work of the sculptor Antony Caro, who I have known for many years.

Artwork can also serve practical purposes. When designing Mezzo, we wanted to include facilities for live music, to acknowledge the site's illustrious past as a venue for performers ranging from Jimi Hendrix to the Sex Pistols. The difficulty was how to hide the stage when it was empty. Our solution was to conceal the extendable stage between performances with vivid, sexy screens by the artist Allan Jones.

Restaurants have often been used as showcases for art. The Ivy features works by Allan Jones, Tom Phillips, Peter Blake, Barry

Flanagan and Eduardo Paolozzi. Eduardo's early work can also be seen at the Neal Street and some Pizza Express restaurants. Pharmacy and Quo Vadis, which make dramatic use of works by Britartists such as Damien Hirst, could be said to be art-led. The Four Seasons in New York has a remarkable Picasso curtain and a massive Bertoia sculpture over the bar. La Colombe d'Or in St Paul de Vence boasts a definitive collection of art dating from the early twentieth century as does the Kronenhalle in Zurich. Some of my favourite art in restaurants is almost accidental – a noodle bar in Tokyo has the dishes on the menu written in calligraphic kanji, on strips of bamboo hanging along the wall. I cannot read Japanese, but it looks wonderful.

During the course of the year I am sent a great deal of information about artists and sculptors, invitations to gallery openings and portfolios from hopefuls. I tend to keep those which are interesting or quirky in a box file so I can retrieve them when I think that a work would suit a particular space. The tailors' dummies, Fat Cow and Lardy Boy, appropriately situated in the entrance to Sartoria, originally came to my attention when I was sent a postcard from the artist just as the restaurant was about to open. I simply couldn't resist the sculptures, though I hope their ample figures have not deterred our customers from sampling the antipasti and risotti on the menu!

The pictures in the Bluebird Club – sultry and slightly decadent images by Jack Vetriano – capture the atmosphere of the period when Malcolm

Campbell was pursuing his land-speed records. I happened to see an advertisement for a forthcoming exhibition at the Portland Gallery on the back of a magazine and arranged to meet Jack, who, enthralled by the Bluebird story, produced seven paintings for the location. The motorcar theme was the inspiration for commissioning the robot-like tightrope walkers, made from salvaged car parts, which balance on the struts in Bluebird Club restaurant. The mobile by Richard Smith, floating within the dramatic roof space at the Bluebird restaurant, is another example of how artwork can complement spatial design and endow personality and character.

Keeping up appearances

Detail is an ongoing process. It only works if the same standards are maintained day after day, year after year. Fresh flowers – so important to first impressions – are sadly the first thing to bite the dust when a restaurant's accountant demands that costs are cut. La Coupole in Paris was memorable for its magnificent, gravity-defying central arrangement; now, however, the flowers have been replaced by a statue of indifferent quality that revolves on its base. Likewise, in Bofinger, where real flowers once bloomed, there are now rather dusty plastic arrangements. A key part of any manager's job is ensuring that the standard of the decoration remains high, walls and doors repaired and damaged items replaced as necessary.

I believe that customers can tell immediately whether a restaurant is well cared for: high standards of maintenance send out the message that customers are also going to be well fed and looked after. There is nothing as off-putting as dusty corners, dirty paintwork, dead flowers, unpolished glasses, littered lavatories and untidy staff – if the management can't get this right, what hope is there for a good meal in relaxed surroundings? It may be a well-worn cliché, but first impressions really do count. Detail – paying close attention to small matters – has a major role in creating an atmosphere that is charming, memorable and, most importantly, gives customers the confidence that they will eat good food and get good service.

Fat Cow and Lardy Boy by Jessica Worrall stand guard at the entrance to Sartoria. These witty takes on a tailor's dummy struck me as perfect for a restaurant in Savile Row, the home of English suit-making.

Café Marly, Paris

Matching the size of the table to the type of restaurant is quite an art. When we came to open Aurora at the Great Eastern Hotel in London we discovered that we had misjudged the size of the tables and chairs, and as a result had to revise down the number of covers we could achieve. In a café or bar, tables need not be very big; but in a smart restaurant people want room to spread out.

Orrery, London

Orrery, London

Salt, Sydney

OVERLEAF LEFT: In de Waag, Amsterdam   OVERLEAF RIGHT: Coast, London

Café Gandolfi, Glasgow

Think only of office politics to realize the significance of a chair.
People will happily perch on a bar-stool for a drink, but many
will want 'something better' if they wish to stay for something
to eat, no matter how casual. Refectory-style seating will be
incredibly sensitive to the price of food, while customers at the
top end of the market invariably demand upholstered chairs of
generous proportions.

Felix, Hong Kong

One Happy Cloud, Stockholm

If there is pure and elevated pleasure in this world it is a **roast pheasant and bread sauce.**

SYDNEY SMITH

Pharmacy, London

Circa, Prince of Wales Hotel, St Kilda, Australia

I find few things more depressing than a faded single bloom (or, worse, plastic flowers) on a restaurant table. Fresh flowers should be just that: fresh. I also think that a big bunch of flowers is one of those luxuries that adds far more value in customers' eyes than they cost to provide. As with so many things, conviction and consistency are equally important: if you are going to make a show of flowers, ensure they are always in peak condition and that they are always there.

Balthazar, New York

Yo! Sushi, London

French House, London

Avenue, London

Wagamama, London

Bank, London

I find few things more depressing than a faded single bloom (or, worse, plastic flowers) on a restaurant table. Fresh flowers should be just that: fresh. I also think that a big bunch of flowers is one of those luxuries that adds far more value in customers' eyes than they cost to provide. As with so many things, conviction and consistency are equally important: if you are going to make a show of flowers, ensure they are always in peak condition and that they are always there.

Balthazar, New York

Yo! Sushi, London

French House, London

Avenue, London

Wagamama, London

Bank, London

Pharmacy, London

Fuel, Sydney

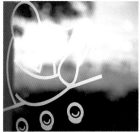

Harry's Dolci, Giudecca

One Happy Cloud, Stockholm

Social, London

Bluebird, London

BANK

Restaurant signs and graphics create expectations even before the customer has set foot through the door. Old-fashioned, modern, trendy, fancy, simple, witty, oblique – the approach of the graphics will do much to set the tone for the restaurant or bar. Colour, too, plays a part, as does the typography. Different restaurants aim to attract different types of customers, and the identity should 'speak' to that particular market, whether it's young or old, male or female, or a more complicated mix.

ZINC

ZINC

Zinc Bar & Grill, London

Belgo Centraal, London

Bar du Grappillon, Paris

Wagamama, London

The Ivy, London

Big Bowl, Chicago

The moment when your waiter hands you the menu signals the true start of the meal. I love those hand-written French bistro menus that have been run off a jelly pad machine with its distinctive purple-blue ink and unforgettable smell. I also prefer straightforward menus to over-complicated ones: if the language is pretentious, it's likely the food will be too.

Simpsons-in-the-Strand, London

Seafood hut, Scarborough

Langan's Brasserie, London

Keith Haring mural, Musée d'Art Moderne café, Antwerp

John Currin pictures on lightboxes, Mash, London

Timna Woollard mural, Cantina del Ponte, London

Restaurateurs may make unlikely art patrons, but they very influential ones nonetheless. From apocryphal tales of Picasso paying for meals by 'doodling' on the tablecloth, restaurateurs have realised the value that art can have in giving a restaurant character and life, whether it's the rainbow-coloured Pop Art of early Pizza Expresses or the YBAs whose work, until recently, adorned the DNA bar at Quo Vadis in Soho. Perhaps the most impressive acts of patronage are the commissions for in situ paintings that really do create (and dictate) the mood of the restaurant.

THE VIDEO BAR
3349 N. Halsted
Chicago

costes

THE JOHN HANCOCK CENTER 875 NORTH MICHIGAN AVENUE CHICAGO, ILLINOIS

The Signature Room
AT THE NINETY-FIFTH

THE RESTAURANT CHICAGO LOOKS UP TO

ZINC
BAR • GRILL

mash

fish!

match
box

R·K·STANLEYS

BLUEBIRD

BANK

Everybody wants a souvenir of a memorable night out – even if they don't smoke.

Vera Mercer photographic montages, Girandole, Park Hyatt, Tokyo

Cary Tamarkin mural, Bryant Park Grill, New York

Monkey Bar, New York

日本料理
つる家
大阪 京都 東京

PARK HYATT TOKYO

Visit the Alternative...

Bar Aqua

NORTH KINGSBURY
CAGO, ILLINOIS 60622

OuStau
DE
BAUMANIÈRE

SOHO HOUSE

BLUE
PRINT
CAFE

BONDST

CENTURY cafe

ELEVEN
MADISON
PARK

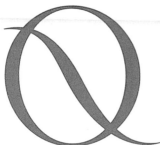

ERY

10

10

Q

301·129

T
Chelsea

ork City

LE PONT DE LA TOUR

ON THE RIVER BY TOWER BRIDGE

A
Z

twist

south beach

PARANOIA
CAFE

up & running

At Jean-Georges in Manhattan, the restaurant service is a model of professionalism: plated food is taken to the pass, approved by the head chef, and only then taken to diners' tables.

Planning and designing a restaurant is just the start of the process: **the real fun begins when you open your doors to paying customers.** Neither does it stop at the opening night. Day after day, night after night, week after week, an amazingly complicated ballet of events takes place: raw ingredients are delivered, prepared, and cooked to order; meals are served in unison, plates are cleared and cleaned, the next course is brought out; wine and water glasses are replenished, bills are kept in check. Moreover, at every single stage there is the potential for something to go wrong. **If good word of mouth is the best recommendation that you can get, then the reverse holds equally true.** Recovering a restaurant's reputation after an appalling experience is even harder work than the daily worries of running the business.

The rewards, however, are great. I can honestly say that **there can be few pleasures to equal the thrill of walking into one's own restaurant and experiencing that animated buzz of people having a good time.** That, for me, and almost certainly for most others involved in the restaurant industry, is what makes it all worthwhile.

The scene is set. The back-of-house fittings and fixtures have been designed, installed and are fully operational. Staff have been trained and briefed. Tables are laid ready for service; china, silver and glassware sparkle; flowers are arranged. Every detail is in place. With the first customers due to arrive, there is a sense of excitement in the air and a certain justifiable feeling of satisfaction. The job, however, has only just begun.

Most of us are familiar with the degree of effort that is required to give a large dinner party. The whole process – deciding on the menu, shopping, preparing the ingredients, cooking, laying the table, serving the food and drinks – takes a good deal of planning, time and energy. Imagine how complicated life would be if you were to serve each guest something different to eat. Then imagine how difficult it would be if your guests arrived at different times and expected their meals to be ready on the table reasonably soon after their arrival. This is the sort of minor miracle successful restaurants perform at least twice a day, up to six or seven days a week, year on year.

It has been estimated that eighty per cent of new restaurants fail within two years of opening. Throughout this book, I have tried to highlight the principal aspects of creating and running a restaurant which must be got right for the enterprise to succeed. But all the care and attention devoted to the design of the space, the choice of location, the selection of the menu, the quality of the food and wine and the training of staff are of little value if no-one decides to come to the restaurant. The challenge is to attract customers from the outset and keep them coming back. Good publicity and a sensible marketing strategy are part of the effort you have to make to survive, but the best possible recommendation is word of mouth from satisfied customers.

It is as well to remember that customers are increasingly sophisticated nowadays. More restaurants are opening, tastes are more exotic, cooking

and food in general have greater media exposure than ever before. The public is better educated in culinary matters than it once was and consequently more demanding. Going out to eat is no longer a once-a-year treat, but a serious alternative to going to the theatre, the cinema or a concert. To please today's exacting customers restaurateurs must consistently meet very high standards.

Establishing a pattern of custom

People eat out for a wide variety of reasons. Celebration still comes high on the list. Birthdays, anniversaries and job promotions are all occasions that we like to mark with a special meal. Increasingly, however, people seek out restaurants for companionship and conviviality. With many of us working in fairly isolated circumstances, often in relative solitude in front of a computer screen, restaurants provide an important way to socialize with others.

While people look to restaurants for entertainment, to provide something new and different, at the same time restaurants can offer the comfort of familiarity – a home from home, a favourite dish that can be enjoyed over and over again. There are many cases of the same customer occupying the same table in a restaurant and ordering the same meal, day in day out, year in year out. Philip Johnson, the famous nonagenarian architect, eats lunch every day at the Four Seasons, a restaurant he designed in 1959. Simone de Beauvoir and Jean Paul Sartre were constant habituées of Aux Deux Magots in Paris, and the late François Mitterrand was often seen at l'Assiette. Years ago I remember noticing plaques above certain tables in St. Pères, a restaurant near Les Halles back in the days when it was still a market. The plaques marked the favoured seats of some of the more successful marchands of the wholesale meat and vegetable business. Dame Barbara Cartland lunches at Claridges most Wednesdays and Lucian Freud

Once established, restaurants start to gather regulars. At Bibendum Oyster Bar, this rather remarkable lady calls by for lunch two or three times a week.

is a well-known frequenter of Sally Clarke's café. The Ivy is famously a haunt of actors, directors, producers and anyone connected with the theatre – there are always one or two paparazzi waiting outside hoping for a snap of some celebrity entering or leaving. In Tokyo, there is a small, simple, family-run noodle bar situated in an impossibly narrow residential street, where from about 11am until 3pm a great convoy of limousines jostle for position, dropping off or picking up Japan's captains of industry.

It takes time, however, to establish a stable pattern of custom, much less such devoted regulars. When I first opened the Neal Street restaurant, we found that on some nights only two tables would be occupied while another restaurant nearby would be full, with a queue of people waiting; on other nights the situation would mysteriously be reversed. I spoke to a friend, a restaurateur of some experience, who told me that it takes a full five years for a restaurant to show an accurate pattern of custom. However, Bibendum, which opened 12 years ago, still has the same customer base it had when it first opened – practically always full.

When a restaurant opens to a great fanfare of media coverage it will temporarily become the hottest spot in town and tables are difficult to get. For a time, such popularity can be self-perpetuating: it's simply human nature that the harder a restaurant is to get into, the more people will want to get into it. There is a danger, however, in being too fashionable, which is going out of fashion. The cutting edge is inherently unstable and the sort of customers who want to be seen in a fashionable place are not always the sort of people who will give you a long-term, stable customer base. Only after there has been a cooling-off period – perhaps when another new restaurant has grabbed the headlines – will a restaurant's core customer base become established.

To have a lasting impact on diners, a restaurant has to offer more than just fashion. It must be attractive in a holistic way, with all the different elements entirely in harmony and balance. The menu should also be priced appropriately. One of the most important elements from the customer's point of view is value for money. If customers feel that they have had a good experience and one that is worth the price they paid for it, then they will surely come back for more.

In the same way as with shops and supermarkets, restaurants increasingly need to develop and maintain a loyal customer base. One way of achieving this can be for restaurants to issue loyalty cards that provide financial and social advantages for their base of regular diners. The notable popularity of Quaglino's bar led to us offering a membership card to regular customers, allowing the holder to shortcut the queue and be the first to be informed of any special events.

Booking

There is something appealing about deciding to go out to eat on the spur of the moment, turning up at a restaurant and finding a table free. Nowadays, however, people increasingly expect to have to book if they are going to be sure of a table in their chosen restaurant. Although larger restaurants can afford to keep a few tables back for what are called 'chances', the economics of the business are such that many smaller places need to ensure that they are as fully booked as possible. Customers, too, appreciate the security of booking ahead, particularly if there will be a large group, or if it is a special occasion.

A full reservation book, however, is no guarantee of success. The bane of the restaurateur's life are the 'no-shows'. Sometimes customers will book several restaurants in advance and then decide which one to go to on the

Big restaurants such as Quaglino's have sophisticated computer booking systems that help them to identify regular customers.

night, forgetting or simply not bothering to cancel the other bookings they have made. Occasionally a reservation may even be confirmed, but the customer still does not turn up. The no-shows are a problem for every restaurant, but for a small business, with 50 tables or fewer, holding a table all evening for diners who do not turn up can make the difference between success and failure. While it is easier to ride that loss in a large restaurant, where a proportion of the diners may turn up on spec to fill the gaps, a few no-shows can cripple a small family restaurant and threaten closure. The prevalence of no-shows explains the rise in the number of restaurants calling to confirm a customer's table on the day. Our restaurants do not keep reservations very far in advance unless it is for a special occasion, such as a Christmas or New Year's Eve party, as we find that this helps reduce the incidence of 'no-shows'.

One solution to this persistant problem might be for restaurateurs to insist on taking a credit card number with the booking, so that if the customer fails to turn up without cancelling a fee can be deducted. Hotels, cinemas and theatres often operate the same type of system; in fact, in many such cases, refunds are not even available on cancellation. Customers would be justifiably infuriated if they booked a table and found that it had been given away to someone else on the night: for the restaurateur the no show amounts to the same thing in reverse.

Another area of some controversy has been the rise in the number of restaurants operating a two-sitting dinner policy, with early diners asked at the time of booking to vacate their tables by 9 p.m. in order to make way for a second sitting. For a restaurateur, this policy does make obvious economic sense. Space represents one of the biggest financial components of the restaurant's balance sheet, and it is sound business practice to make the most effective use of it.

Nevertheless, the practice of having two evening sittings has developed largely in response to customer demand and follows the general pattern of eating out. Although a few customers do like to come early and stay late, most fall into either the early or late camp. Some people going to the cinema or theatre want to eat before, while others like to eat afterwards. Americans generally prefer to eat much earlier than Europeans. Families often opt for an earlier time than young people who intend to make a night of it. Ensuring that early diners are aware that they *may* have to give up their table at a set time protects the later diner – it is highly frustrating to arrive at a restaurant only to be told you have to wait for your table.

Many large restaurants have opted for an electronic booking system, rather than a reservations book. These systems are expensive to install and maintain, the required staff training demands a large investment of time and effort and it can be hugely frustrating when the system 'goes down', as invariably happens from time to time. Unless the restaurant has in excess of 200 covers, keeping a big reservations book beside the telephone should be perfectly sufficient.

For a large restaurant, the advantages of an electronic booking system outweigh the disadvantages. The restaurateur will know how many covers to expect and can adjust the staff and purchase of raw materials accordingly; a database of regular customers can be maintained and several receptionists can take bookings at the same time. When we opened Quaglino's, handling the flood of telephone bookings was a nightmare. With four or five people trying to manage the reservation book all at once, a computerized system was urgently required. At that time there was no restaurant-specific software available. Wendy Hendricks, the assistant restaurant manager, worked very closely with a computer programmer to write a programme that we have subsequently used in all our large restaurants; indeed it has since been adopted by other restaurateurs.

Publicity and marketing

No matter to what degree each might complain about the other, restaurateurs and reviewers are locked in a symbiotic relationship. Both sides need each other. When a restaurant first opens, reviews serve to bring customers through the door for the first time. Later, when the restaurant becomes established, follow-up reviews can provide a useful reminder of a restaurant's special qualities or appeal. In turn, reviews and features about new restaurants serve as a way of filling pages and assuaging the media's constant thirst for novelty.

There is certainly a place for informed and intelligent criticism in the restaurant trade. A well-respected and knowledgeable reviewer, who has a thorough understanding of the way the business works and no personal axe to grind, provides an invaluable service for both restaurateurs and customers alike. The power of the reviewer, however, tends to be somewhat exaggerated. Most restaurant critics would be among the first to admit that bad reviews rarely close restaurants. Restaurants close because they fail their customers, who vote with their feet and don't go back. On the other hand, a good review can bring a hitherto overlooked restaurant to the attention

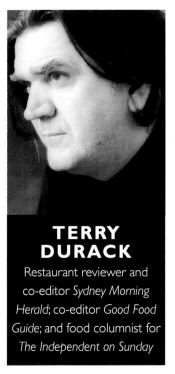

TERRY DURACK

Restaurant reviewer and co-editor *Sydney Morning Herald*; co-editor *Good Food Guide*; and food columnist for *The Independent on Sunday*

All restaurateurs want good reviews. Here's how to increase your chances of getting one. First, find out what your friendly neighbourhood restaurant reviewer looks like. You can do this by subtly checking out the back of everyone's neck for that tell-tale **666** mark, or by looking for twin protuberances under the hair on the top of the head. However, it's probably easier simply to check out the picture at the top of the restaurant review column in the newspaper, or to ask your fellow restaurateurs for a detailed description.

Then, wait. You won't know when the critics are coming, because they will – or should – book under assumed names. Therefore you will always have to run your restaurant as well as you possibly can. If this is difficult, may I respectfully suggest another long-term career option?

Running your restaurant as well as you can is also the best way of being considered for a review in the first place. The worst way is to ring or write to reviewers and suggest that their lives would be changed for the better if they just came to their senses and visited your establishment. Whenever I am solicited by a restaurateur, that particular restaurant automatically goes to the bottom of my pile. Send a current menu by all means, with a business card and relevant details in a covering letter, but don't call us. We'll call you.

Now that you know who the critics are, there is one thing you must do. Forget it. When a restaurant critic walks in the door, do not drop what you are carrying – I can always tell when I am spotted by the amount of cutlery that hits the floor. Nor should you fawn, faint or fall to your knees and cross yourself. We're not worth it. Critics don't come to your restaurant to see how critics are treated. They come to find out how their readers will be treated.

Do not make a reviewer's order look 'special'. A prawn entrée once came to me as 12 perfect specimens arranged in concentric circles on a bed of pristine baby leaves, while at the next table, the same dish came as five prawns thrown from a great height. I reviewed that dish, not mine.

Do not hang around the table relating the intimate details of your restaurant's progress to reviewers. Only your bank manager is fascinated by the fact that Tuesdays are slow, Wednesdays are so-so, but Fridays are fabulous and Saturday nights are what make it all worthwhile.

Do not throw away the first entrée you have cooked for a reviewer in order to do another, more perfect one. A less-than-perfect entrée served on time will always rate higher than a perfect one that arrives an hour later.

Do not send out unsolicited dishes. Most critics take care to select a properly balanced order and resent the intrusion. It is also a scientifically proven fact that restaurateurs have an innate ability to choose the last dish in the world that a restaurant critic feels like eating. Often, it is the worst dish on the menu.

Do not make excuses for everything that happens. Noticing my dish of uneaten (and inedible) lamb in a highly rated London restaurant, the owner was quick to explain that it was the wrong time of the year for lamb. Tell me about it.

Do not tell the critic that tonight is the last night of the current menu. It doesn't matter. For hundreds of years, people have been dining at restaurants on the last night of a particular menu without any adverse side effects.

Do not offer critics a free meal. If they are reputable, it is their duty to pay. If they are not, their review is worthless.

What do you do? The most important thing is to make sure that you are ready for the critics when they do come. Make sure that your chef, your waiters and your dishwasher are ready to do their best; that you have the best produce you can afford; and that the restaurant is a welcoming, relaxed and enjoyable place, at all times. The best way to ensure that, of course, is to practise on your customers.

of a wider public. There have been many instances of small, local restaurants experiencing a dramatic upturn in their fortunes after a positive notice appeared in a national newspaper.

Fear of bad reviews and contempt for reviewers in general can lead to restaurateurs either bending over backwards to please a critic or reacting in a confrontational or combative way. Most good critics go to great lengths to preserve their anonymity, so that they can report on the experience of eating out in a particular restaurant from the standpoint of the ordinary customer. Nevertheless, word does get about and critics are often recognized despite their aliases. The worst thing a restaurateur can do in such circumstances is to give the critic special treatment: over-attentive service can backfire, with the service itself being singled out for criticism. At the other extreme, no matter how provocative a critic might be, it is important not to rise to the bait. A couple of years ago, a notoriously quick-tempered chef ejected a critic famous for his scathing reviews from his restaurant and banned him from eating there ever again. The episode attracted a great deal of publicity, but it is doubtful whether it did the chef or his restaurant any favours in the long run.

Bad reviews do hurt, and especially if they are based on a hasty or ill-informed appraisal. While a bad review may be taken with a pinch of salt by readers who realize it is just one person's opinion, the morale of kitchen and waiting staff can suffer as a result. All restaurants have off-nights; however critics with an understanding of the business will be able to tell the difference between the occasional slip-up and problems that are indicative of more serious shortcomings. A new restaurant will invariably have teething troubles and will take some time to settle down; responsible critics generally revisit after a reasonable period of time has elapsed before sitting in judgement. Unfortunately, restaurants do often get reviewed before the first tooth has even appeared.

The ever-increasing numbers of restaurants has been matched by a similar proliferation of guidebooks. From the well-established bibles such as the Michelin and Gault Millau guides, the marketing tools of AA, Cellnet and Courvoisier, to the consumer-led *Time Out*, *Good Food Guide* and *Zagat Survey*, the would-be diner faces a bewildering choice. The situation is complicated by the fact that guidebooks rarely base their recommendations on the same criteria, with listings organized variously by price, cuisine and geography. Unlike a review in a magazine or newspaper, a guidebook listing may well be out of date by the time the book is published.

The famous Michelin guide originally arose as a canny piece of marketing. Back in the early days of motoring, the entrepreneurial Michelin brothers, French tyre manufacturers, were seeking a means of promoting the whole concept of driving as a leisure activity: more journeys would mean more tyre sales. To reinforce the link between motoring and pleasure they came up with the idea of a guide to restaurants and watering holes that intrepid motorists could visit with the aid of maps and route-planners. Employing the famous critic Curnonsky to write reviews, under the pseudonym 'Bibendum', the first few guides included Algeria and Tunisia as well as France. After a five-year interruption during the First World War, the guide in the 800-page format we know today was published in 1920. The first star was awarded in 1926, the two- and three-star ratings date from 1931 in the case of provincial France, 1933 for Paris. From that point the guide expanded to other countries, and is now considered by some to be the gastro-tourist's bible. While many feel that over the last decade or so the criteria for awarding Michelin stars and knife-and-fork ratings have not kept up with the times, there have been some signs of change – pub food has made an appearance and the guide recently broke with tradition and awarded three stars to one chef for each of his two restaurants.

Other guides rely less on the authority of an unnamed 'inspector' or critic and more on feedback from customers. In a recently published *Zagat Survey* of London restaurants, 1,000 restaurants were nominated by respondents. Some 2,500 people took the trouble to complete the survey – itself quite a feat – as the survey comprised several pages of restaurants, alphabetically listed and with minuscule columns for comment and opinion. The fact that so many people found the time to fill in the questionnaire indicates the increasing levels of interest in restaurants as a whole.

Restaurants can wait to be reviewed and surveyed, or they can engage more actively in the process. While a celebrity chef such as Marco Pierre White might declare that he has no need of a press office, most larger restaurants today take a more positive view of marketing and promotion. Word of mouth is important and good reviews are always welcome, but in today's competitive market restaurants are foolish simply to sit back and hope for the best. Good marketing can help a restaurant attract customers not merely at peak times, but in traditionally quieter periods as well.

In larger establishments, it is an advantage to employ someone who is experienced in dealing with the press and can relieve the burden on the rest of the staff. We get enquiries from all over the world, requests which

have ranged from a Tokyo-based design magazine wanting to feature Quaglino's interior to a German financial publication needing figures on the restaurants' turnovers. Sometimes a fashion magazine will want to use a restaurant for a shoot or a television programme may want to use a bar as a location for a scene in a drama series. In addition, the food press often ring looking for a comment or a response to a current news item. The press office can field all these calls and requests and refer them to the relevant department or person.

In the context of restaurants, marketing must be exceptionally subtle. It is very easy to alienate regular diners and put off prospective customers with anything that resembles a hard sell. Successful promotions often take the form of special offers, usually organized in conjunction with a newspaper, where meals are available for a lower fixed price upon presentation of tokens or vouchers collected from the tie-in publication. One of our most successful promotions was a special lunch menu at Quaglino's that was offered for the duration of the Royal Academy's blockbuster art exhibition, Monet in the Twentieth Century; Mezzo ran a similar promotion to tie in with the Soho Jazz Festival. Such promotions tend to run in the typically quiet times of January, February and August, or in connection with a sympathetic event.

Other useful marketing devices we have employed include an address book, detailing the addresses, telephone numbers and contact names of the various restaurants and shops within the collection, which is handed out with the bills and available in the shops, and, more ambitiously, a magazine Live It, featuring food-related articles and recipes from a number of the restaurants' chefs. The marketing department also composes a newsletter for internal circulation which goes out four times a year. Like many other enterprises, we also have our own website, which is likely to develop into a sophisticated tool for communication and marketing in the future.

The marketing department really comes into its own in the run-up to the opening of a new restaurant. Before the launch, the press have to be briefed and a press pack produced, which means that photography of the restaurant, the staff, the kitchen and the food has to be commissioned and supervised. During this period we organize meals for our employees as well as half-price lunches and dinners to help with staff training. In addition to the official opening, we generally throw a launch party for friends and family, and all these events need coordinating with the management and kitchen. Once the restaurant is up and running, the marketing department can then also conduct low-key customer surveys in order to pinpoint areas of satisfaction and dissatisfaction, informal information gathering that serves as useful means for the restaurateur to check the pulse of the business and put right any deficiencies.

Scams

The restaurant has been successfully launched, the press has been largely favourable and you are beginning to attract a steady stream of regular customers. But your figures are not quite as good as you would have hoped. What could be going wrong?

One possibility is theft. Restaurant theft can take many forms; it can be perpetrated by customers as well as staff. And unless you control it, you will find it hard to break even, much less make a profit. Economies of scale dictate that even a small degree of pilfering repeated often enough can add up to a substantial loss.

In a recent article in The New Yorker, Anthony Bourdain, a chef and former restaurant-owner, mentioned that he had heard of a survey of the American prison population which reportedly found that of all the former occupations quoted by inmates, by far the most common was 'cook'. Of course, such findings do not indicate an inherent tendency to criminality

Satisfied customers generate good word-of-mouth – quite the best form of advertising there is, and not something you can buy.

among restaurant staff, but they do highlight the fact that the restaurant business does offer considerable scope for what might be called 'dirty tricks'.

The reasons for this are perfectly understandable. The vast majority of successful restaurants operate at a hectic pace and it can be difficult for management to keep an eye on every single member of staff every single minute of a shift. Unlike clothes shops where products can be electronically tagged, or retail outlets with their close circuit televisions and store detectives, restaurants sell consumable items which can be difficult to monitor. Then, again, the temptations are significant. In an upmarket restaurant, quite large sums of money will very probably change hands over the course of an evening, some of it in cash, and there are considerable profits to be made from even small-scale deceptions.

By far the most common type of restaurant theft among staff is simply eating or drinking what they're supposed to be serving. High wastage levels in the kitchen may indicate that some of the staff have developed a taste for their own food. Some thirsty waiters have been known to ring up a drink from the bar, consume it quickly at the waiter's station and then, before the bill is presented to the customer, ask the manager to have the item deleted from the bill because of a 'spill' or some similar excuse. One waiter who carried this scam too far got so drunk that he literally had to be carried out of the restaurant.

As is the case in many businesses, toilet rolls and cleaning products often have a tendency to walk. More serious losses include glassware, cutlery and plates. There is a story of one maître d'hotel, who had worked for many of London's top restaurants during the course of his career. Guests invited to dinner at his house would be asked where they would like to eat – the Dorchester? Langan's? The maître d' could lay a table for 12 in complete sets of different crockery and cutlery that had been stolen from many of his former employers.

Because the profit margins are generally higher for alcohol than food, the bar offers many opportunities for those seeking to make easy money and this is the area most susceptible to theft. The classic scam is for a barman to bring in spirits from cheaper sources outside and sell measures from his own bottles at the restaurant's standard price, then keeping the difference. Refinements of the same basic dodge include passing off inferior alcohol or wine in place of a named brand or good vintage; watering down the booze; topping up bottles of mineral water with tap water; taking cash payments for drinks, pocketing them, and bringing in empty bottles to cover any stocktaking discrepancy; or simply taking the stock to sell on in other venues.

Unscrupulous chefs have their own tricks. Accepting higher prices or short deliveries from suppliers, in exchange for a backhander, is one widespread kitchen scam. Dishonest managers have been known to slip a false name on to the payroll and pocket the wages of the ficticious employee. Credit card fraud is also common, while cash transactions present an ever-present temptation.

In recent years, electronic systems, such as Remanco and Micros, have made things a little more difficult for the dedicated restaurant thief, but even electronic systems can be beaten. The lesson is that all restaurant managers and owners have to keep a close eye on their stock, credit card and cash transactions. Spot checks of bags and lockers are an important safeguard. Stock can be marked and levels monitored over a period of time to detect unusual discrepancies and deliveries can be double-checked to see that you get what you are charged for.

As if all this was not enough to worry about, from time to time you are bound to come across a few customers trying to get in on the act. Fairly recently there has been a spate of dry-cleaning scams. A customer will write in to complain that a waiter has spilled something on his or her clothing, enclose a receipt for cleaning and ask for reimbursement. Often no record

Some chairs stack better than others!

can be found of the person ever having dined at the restaurant. Equally easy to spot are those 'customers' who put in complaints about their treatment at Sunday lunch, when the restaurant in question was not actually open for lunch that day.

In response to the number of complaints we were regularly receiving relating to stomach upsets from eating oysters, we put a 'health warning' on our menus, advising against the eating of shellfish in conjunction with the drinking of spirits. This was prompted by the evidence, revealed by our copies of bills, that many of those complaining of food poisoning had actually had quite alarming amounts to drink before, during and after eating their meal, and thus that their symptoms could more accurately be ascribed to hangovers. There has been a marked decrease in such complaints ever since.

But full marks for cheek must go to a well-dressed gentleman who came into one of our restaurants and proceded to order a three-course meal with champagne. After he had finished, he called for the manager and asked him to ring the police, confessing that he did not have enough money to pay for his meal. The customer explained that he did this sort of thing all the time and the police would know who he was. The manager politely declined his request and instead relieved the man of his wallet and watch by way of recompense.

The future

To be successful in the long term, all businesses, and restaurants are no exception, have to anticipate trends. Inspired guesswork comes into it, and so does keeping well informed about current developments. In some cases, staying ahead of the game can mean setting a trend yourself: people do not always know what they want until they are offered it. One of the most encouraging aspects of the restaurant business is that there is always scope for improvement and innovation.

Restaurants have changed beyond all recognition over the last decade. London, San Francisco, Hong Kong, Los Angeles and New York have led the way with the introduction of new, innovative styles of cooking and clean, modern styles of restaurant design. French restaurants, which were formerly in the culinary vanguard, have been slow to catch up with these developments. The old kitchen hierarchies, a heavy reliance on traditional techniques and a culinary culture that is based on striving after quality stars, diplomas, medals and awards has meant that modernism has been ignored to some extent in France and outside influences and trend developments have been very largely neglected. The overall result of this has been to hold back the middle ground, although despite this France still reigns supreme at the three-star or *haute cuisine* level.

Top Parisian chefs are just starting to experiment with culinary mixes – Pierre Gagnaire was awarded three stars by Michelin a few years ago for cooking that is certainly a couple of steps beyond the classic tradition. Alain Ducasse has broken the mould with his Parisian restaurant Spoon Food and Wine. Not only is the menu written in English with French subtitles, but the dishes represent a considerable departure from the classic French cuisine with which he made his name; what's even more heretical is the fact that his wine list is only 20 per cent French in origin, with the rest deriving from other European and New World growers.

In London there is a trend for more and more restaurants to move towards specialization. This does not merely relate to a particular ethnic style but also within a single type of dish. Just as many Japanese restaurants focus on teppanyaki, sushi or shabu-shabu, we now have places serving variations on the fairly limited themes of sausage and mash, or mussels, chips and beer. My old Soup Kitchen idea is staging a comeback, with the new soup-based lunch places such as Soup Opera giving Prêt à Manger a run for their money. I suspect this trend – the restaurant equivalent of niche marketing – will continue to grow in the future.

The food revolution has had an immense impact on people's expectations of restaurants; *Zagat Survey* noted that their respondents were eating out more than they were three years ago: last year, in Britain alone, people spent £3 billion on eating out. This desire to eat out in pleasant surroundings will survive whatever economic vicissitudes lie in the future. Our experience of opening Quaglino's in the depth of a recession suggests there is no need for restaurateurs to be paralysed by an economic downturn, provided a careful eye is kept on the cost base. The essential thing to remember is not to shave costs to such an extent that you lose the whole impulse of a place. Even when life is gloomy, restaurants can still do good business: people may spend a little less, but they always have a need to meet with people and cheer themselves up.

It is undoubtedly harder for first-time restaurateurs to break into the business or for small restaurants to survive and this trend looks set to continue. In most major cities, property prices are at a premium, which squeezes out the neighbourhood restaurants serving local customers. New legislation has also added to the start-up costs. At the same time, I think we're going to see more small restaurants open in provincial towns and rural areas, away from the bustle of urban life. I know several people – like an insurance salesman who has made a quiet success of his 40-seater restaurant – who have opted to change both career and locale and wonder why they didn't do it years ago.

In cities there will be a further strengthening of the links between retail outlets and restaurants. There have always been places to eat in large department stores but it is interesting to note that Selfridges, after its recent revamp, now offers no fewer than twelve eating opportunities – an oyster bar, salt beef sandwich joint, Espresso café, Premier, Dome, an Italian restaurant, a wine bar, three coffee shops, a large food court and Yo! Sushi. This approach really equates to a case of having a variety of restaurants with a shop attached.

Similarly, the world's great hotels have always had their own dining rooms. The Crillon in Paris has Les Ambassadeurs, possibly the most elegant dining room in the world, Raffles in Singapore boasts several sumptuous restaurants, and The Connaught's famous dining room is enduringly popular with businessmen and well-heeled tourists. What's new today is the desire to attract an increasing number of non-residents and to give hotel restaurants their own identity distinct from the hotel. In London, there is the Metropolitan with Nobu as its main dining room, and Vong and La Tante Claire at the Berkeley. Daniel in New York has moved into the Surrey Suite Hotel, and Cirque 2000 is installed in the New York Palace Hotel. The restaurant in Tokyo's Shinjuku Park Hyatt, the New York Bar and Grill, is one of the best in the area, while Kable's in Sydney's Regent Hotel demonstrates the fact that relaxed modern style can work in a sector traditionally dominated by *haute cuisine*.

How restaurants evolve in the coming years depends to a large extent on the young people who will be the owners, staff, chefs and customers of the future. Despite the fact that cooking is not given much weight in the school curriculum, and that in many of today's homes shared family mealtimes seem to be a thing of the past, many young people display a keen interest in both cooking and food. This interest is revealed in the growing numbers applying to catering colleges and cookery schools and given impetus by the fact that all kinds of restaurant work are increasingly seen as aspirational careers. Legislation which has outlawed the punishing hours which employees used to work together with better working conditions is bound to encourage more into the business.

The kitchen at Mezzo divides into different workstations where everyone has a specific role.

Taking the plunge

If you are not disheartened by the statistics, dismayed by the risks, put off by the challenges or daunted by the regulations, the restaurant business can be uniquely satisfying. It's complicated, fraught with difficulty and constantly changing. Yet of all the enterprises with which I have been involved over the last half century, from design to retail, the restaurant business has consistently given me the most pleasure. A magical blend of people, food, wine, glamour, hard work, exhilaration, exhaustion and reward, I find it simply irresistible.

In conclusion, I can only offer some basic advice to those seeking to take the plunge:

Keep it simple There's no point in stretching resources for the sake of complication and this applies to every aspect of a restaurant – the location, the interior, the menu, the service.

Be flexible Don't tie yourself to a fixed idea or concept. Even with many years of experience, it is still necessary to be flexible and to adapt approaches where necessary. Write your menu daily or weekly; buy what is available and seasonal.

Never compromise on quality Make your mark with at least a couple of specialities. It is better to have a few really good dishes that you are known for than try to manage a huge selection of indifferent ones.

Be prepared to seek advice The business is a continuous learning curve. Even those who have been involved in restaurants for years have much to learn.

Take care of your staff They are your most important asset and the lifeline to your success. Involve them in the business, be kind and considerate and keep them briefed and motivated.

Take care of your customers Keep them coming back; make sure they are getting good service, a good meal and good value for money.

Good restaurants are all about passion, dedication and conviction. Hang on to your enthusiasm and it will make the hard work worthwhile.

Countdown to an opening

The opening of a restaurant demands careful organization. There must be enough time in the programme to brief and train all staff properly and get all systems working smoothly. On the other hand, there is the need to avoid paying excessive overheads before the restaurant opens and begins to earn its keep. Tight scheduling and strategic planning are called for to ensure everything goes well on the night.

The location and size of the venture will dictate whether the opening will be marked by a small, low-key party with a few invited journalists and friends or alternatively consist of a series of parties with a higher media profile. Here is the countdown to the opening of our first restaurant in Paris, Alcazar, which required particularly sensitive handling, due to the high degree of media interest.

Minus 16 WEEKS
• Terence Conran, David Loewi, managing director of the Conran restaurants, and Michel Besmond, general manager of Alcazar, appoint chef, Guillaume Lutard.
• Guillaume Lutard goes to work in other Conran restaurant kitchens – Bluebird, Quaglino's and Cantina. He visits Rorgue, the foundry which is making the stove for the kitchen, and advises on its specification.
• Michel Besmond works with the general manager at Quaglino's and Bluebird. He starts to interview his key senior staff and appoints his restaurant manager. Wendy Hendricks, personnel trainer at Bluebird, is seconded to Alcazar.
• Weekly progress meetings are set up.

15 WEEKS
• Guillaume Lutard, Michel Besmond, David Loewi and Terence Conran discuss the menu and decide on a list of dishes. Dates are arranged for tastings.

• IT systems are ordered and samples of tableware, linen, glasses and cutlery are requisitioned for table-top presentation.

12 WEEKS
• The general manager starts recruiting and interviewing the remainder of the key staff, and the chef starts to recruit his team for the kitchen.
• Terence Conran, Michel Besmond, Guillaume Lutard and Wendy Hendricks attend the purchasing manager's table-top presentation. The graphics, linens and uniforms are considered and the decision is made on which items will carry the restaurant's logo.
• Final decisions are made on which articles of cookware and cutlery, plates and glasses, cruets, napkins and uniforms to order.

11 WEEKS
• Orders are placed and delivery schedules are arranged.

10 WEEKS
• The senior sous chef and assistant manager start.
• The Remanco and reservations systems are delivered off-site and wired up; primary IT training is instigated.
• The restaurant systems and procedures are set up.

9 WEEKS
• The health and safety consultants are briefed and give their recommendations.
• The delivery schedule is finalized.

8 WEEKS
• Further staff are interviewed and recruited.
• The first press releases are distributed to targeted media.

7 WEEKS
• The sequence of service is prepared and explained by Michel Besmond and Wendy Hendricks, and by Guillaume Lutard along with his head sous chef.
• From the sequence of service, the induction manual is prepared for the front-of-house staff, covering table plans, table numbering, how the service stations work and other vital information.
• The induction manual is then prepared for the kitchen staff. This outlines the flow of service ranging from the delivery of goods, to the preparation, the *mise en place* and the cooking of each dish. The induction manuals are then mailed out to the successful recruits.

6 WEEKS

• The full press packs and some press invitations are sent out.

• French press are briefed. *Madame Figaro*, *Elle Deco* and *Maison Marie Claire* arrange food shoots at Terence Conran's apartment.

5 WEEKS

• Half-price preview mailings go out to targeted Conran Shop Paris customers.

• Press party invitations go out.

• Opening party invitations go out.

4 WEEKS

• Second phase of the IT training starts.

• Ovens are polished and commissioned.

3 WEEKS

• Possession of the restaurant.

• Senior kitchen staff and pastry chef start.

• Senior kitchen staff and administration staff move over from Head Office.

• The head sommelier, head barman and head receptionist start.

• The first deliveries of china, glass, linen, cutlery and furniture arrive.

• Artworks are installed.

2 WEEKS

• The remainder of the staff start.

• Induction days start in the kitchen and front-of-house.

• IT and systems training.

• Waiters stations are commissioned.

• Mock services are initiated.

• Service routes are taped on to the floor.

• Front-of-house and kitchen staff are familiarized with the Remanco system.

• The kitchen preps and cooks every dish on the menu, fine-tuning as they go.

DAY 10

• Terence Conran, David Loewi and Michel Besmond have a tasting of the full menu, and make notes.

• Menu debriefing with Terence Conran, David Loewi and Guillaume Lutard.

• The menu packs are distributed with descriptions of each dish. Possible allergens, such as nuts and certain oils are flagged.

DAY 7

• The reservations booking system kicks in.

• Half the staff and their invited guests practise lunch.

• Wine tastings with Bill Baker and the sommeliers are held, as well as cigar tastings.

• The other half of staff and their guests practise dinner.

• Staff debriefing to highlight any problems.

DAY 6

• Lunch and dinner for Conran Shop staff.

• Tastings of cheeses, caviar, *foie gras* and any unusual dishes on the menu are organized by the suppliers for the waiting staff.

• Another staff debriefing.

• Terence Conran makes final decisions on details such as vases and flowers.

DAY 5

• The invited press get a tour of the restaurant with lunch and a full press pack.

• Another staff debriefing.

• Press party and dinner.

DAY 4

• Fine-tuning the staff training.

• Full staff debriefing.

• Opening night party.

DAY 3

• Half-price lunch and dinner for invited members of the public.

• Another full staff debriefing.

DAY 2

• Penultimate tweaking of service.

• Half-price dinner.

DAY 1

• Half-price lunch.

• Final staff debriefing.

OPENING DAY

Never underestimate the number of tasks that will need doing each and every day.

People come to different restaurants for different reasons at different times of the day or different days of the week. The trick is to ensure that your own restaurant appeals to enough people enough of the time. That's not to say you should try to be all things to all men: I like to think that a restaurant run with conviction (and a sensible business plan) will draw in exactly the type of people it is aimed at; just hold your nerve and accept that if you are running a restaurant that appeals to twenty-somethings looking for somewhere to drink and grab a bite to eat, it's unlikely that their parents are going to want to go there!

Restaurant, Bruges

Jean-Georges, New York

Bar de Montins, Creuse

Café, Paris

Lunch, Pontypridd

Lunch, New York

Skala Bar, Vienna

There's nothing like a good 'buzz' to generate
business. I could never understand the appeal
of those hushed restaurants where the food
was brought to the table as if to the altar of a
lady-chapel – surely one of the marks of a
good restaurant should be the sound of
people having a good time?

The Cow, London

Great Eastern Dining Room, London

Wagamama, London

The opening night of a restaurant signals the final stage of all the various planning, designing, briefing, ordering and training stages. If all goes well, this is the time when these different elements are brought to successful fruition under the eyes of the attending public and the scrutiny of the critics.

Berns, Stockholm

The New York Times, Dining Out

Jonathan Meades review, *The Times*, London

The ways in which we decide upon a restaurant are many. Given the choice, I suspect most of us prefer personal recommendation from someone whose opinions and tastes we trust. But visitors to a town or city, or people wanting to go to a restaurant for a special occasion, are likely to research their choice more thoroughly – which is where guides and critics come in. In the early days of opening, a good review can make a restaurant, whilst a savage one may close it before it's ever properly up and running. Of course, a review will probably be based on a single meal, although it may have been uncharacteristically good or bad; the huge challenge for a restaurant is to deliver the best it can at each and every service.

Saveur magazine

Vogue Entertaining & Travel magazine, Australia

Michelin Guide, France

Zagat Survey   2000

Fuel, Sydney

'Synergy' is one of the key marketing concepts of our time, it seems. At Fuel in Sydney and Bluebird in London, this translates into a group of sympathetic businesses all in the same place: bar, café, restaurant, take-away... although where the MG cars fit in, I'm not quite sure! At Bluebird, the forecourt is modelled on a small market square in France – somewhere selling fresh fruit, vegetables and flowers, with a café spilling out on to the pavement.

Bluebird, London

A restaurant is . . . your first date; a candlelit dinner for two; a no-expense-spared blow-out on your 50th birthday; a celebration of the senses; a stage-set on which everything happens by magic; the conclusion to a tragic love affair. Or a dream come true?

batterie de cuisine

Alcarraza A porous earthenware vessel for cooling drinks.
Antimacassar Protective covering for chair backs.

Back of house The kitchens and any part of the restaurant not seen by the customer.
Bain marie Hot water bath for keeping food warm.
Banquette Built-in wall sofa, normally padded.
Barista Trained coffee maker.
Bord-de-plat Protects the border of a dish on which sauce is being served.
Braising pan Oval or rectangular two-handled pan with well-fitting lid.
Brat pan For making large amounts of soups, stews or stocks.

Ça marche Traditionally called by the chef to signify that an order has been recorded.
Cabaret A pedestal table from which drinks may be served.
Chafing dish For cooking at table – a pan over a portable source of heat.
Chef de partie Ensures the smooth running of one section of the kitchen, such as the sauce, pastry, or larder areas, and usually supervises junior staff.
Chef de rang Serves drinks (not wine if there is a sommelier) and food, and takes dessert orders.
Chinois Fine mesh strainer for soups, sauces, stocks etc.
Cloche Convex dish cover for keeping food hot.
Cocotte Small, round ovenproof earthenware dishes.
Cold rooms Storage for goods requiring refrigeration.
Commis chef Assists with daily mis-en-place requirements.

Commis waiter Carries food from the kitchen to waiter stations and does general, menial jobs.
Crêpe pan Shallow, flat-bottomed pan for cooking crêpes.

Dariol moulds For making pastry items.
Diable A cooking pot consisting of two pans, one forming a lid over the other.
Dispense bar Bar for restaurant use.
Dolle well Insulated crustacea display shelf.
Dry stores Storage for dried goods.

Ecailler The person who opens shellfish.

Front of house The main restaurant.

Gastronorm Specially designed trays that slot straight into storage fridge, dry store etc.
General manager Responsible for the entire restaurant operation.
Gueridon Serving table, pedestal or trolley.

Head chef Responsible for managing kitchen and all kitchen staff, and producing menus.
Head waiter Takes customer orders and is responsible for a specific area of the restaurant.
Humidor For keeping cigars moist.

Kitchen porter Washes up, cleans back of house areas and assists chefs.

Lobster crackers For breaking open lobsters.

Maitre d'Hôtel The person in charge of the dining room.
Mandolin Sharp gauged tool for very thin slicing.
Marmite Earthenware pot, glazed on the inside.
Meat bat Used for making escalopes of veal, chicken etc.

Mis-en-place All activities which prepare for the serving of food.
Mouli-légume For making a vegetable purée.

Palladin Large cylindrical rubbish bin on wheels.
Papilotte Paper frill used to garnish the bone-end of meat.
Pass Where food is sent from kitchen to restaurant upon completion of dish.
Pastry docker For pricking pastry.
Piano (also called range) Main cooking stove.
Poêlon A small, long-handled saucepan.

Rotisserie For cooking with a spit.
Runner General dogsbody who carries trays of food and dirty crockery to and from the kitchen.

Salamander High-level grill.
Samovar A kettle that constantly supplies hot water.
Sauté pan Round pan, deeper than a frying pan.
Servery For storing items of table service and preparing certain dishes.
Sommelier Responsible for the wine list and the serving and recommending of wine.
Sous chef Assists head chef in overseeing and directing all aspects of kitchen operations.
Stock pot Very large pan for making stocks.

Tronc The money distributed to staff from the service charge.

Waiter station The area where customer food is brought prior to serving and where dirty crockery is collected by runners.
Waiter's friend Pocket corkscrew and bottle opener.
Wine cellar Temperature controlled area for storing wine.

index

Page numbers in *italic* refer to captions to illustrations; those in **bold** highlight featured contributors.

acknowledgements

With grateful thanks to Simon Willis whose expertise, enthusiasm and critical eye have been invaluable at every stage of development; also thanks to the other members of the creative team for their respective contributions – Helen Lewis, Nadine Bazar and Liz Wilhide. Thanks are also due to Jamie Abbott, Richard Atkinson, Denny Hemming, Bernice Langton and Kelly Luchford.

The publisher thanks the following photographers and organizations for their kind permission to reproduce the photographs in this book:
1 Georgia Glynn-Smith; 2 *Marie Claire Maison*/Dana Gallagher/Marion Kalt; 3 Tim Street-Porter; 4 Jason Lowe; 6 Aquarius Library; 7 Bart von Leuven/Restaurant De Pastorie, Lichtaart in Belgium/from Chefs Privé published by Standaard Publishers; 8 above left Diaf/Camille Moirenc; 8 above centre Explorer/A Wolf; 8 above right Christian Sarramon; 8 centre left Michael Busselle; 8 centre Christian Sarramon; 8 centre right Gilles Rigoulet; 8 below left Christian Sarramon; 8 below centre Agence Top/J F Tripelon/M J Jarry; 8 below right AKG London/Himan B Hurlbut Collection at Cleveland Museum of Art; 10 Hulton Getty; 11 Christian Sarramon; 13 Gilles Rigoulet; 15 AKG London; 16 Agence Top/Pascal Hinous; 18 Museum of the City of New York/The Byron Collection; 19 Magnum/Sergio Larrain; 20 Explorer/F Chauzot; 21 Gilles Rigoulet; 22 Rapho/Fouad Elkhoury; 24–25 Magnum/Henri Cartier-Bresson; 26 gettyone stone/Roger Brooks; 28 Topham Picturepoint; 29 Marianne Majerus; 30 Georgia Glynn-Smith; 31 Arcaid/Chris Gascoigne; 32–33 Aude Vincent/Mariette Landon & Associés; 35 David Loftus; 39 Pizza Express/Keith Hunter; 40 left Hémisphères/Bertrand Rieger; 40 right The Image Bank/Kay Chernush; 41 above left Arcaid/Nicholas Kane/architect Mark Newson; 41 above right © Wagamama Ltd./Alan Sheldon; 41 below left Miriam Bleeker/courtesy of Architektur & Wohnen; 41 below right View/Chris Gascoigne; 42 left Debbie Patterson; 42 below right Jean Cazals; 42–43 Tom Birmingham; 43 below Christian Sarramon; 44 Christian Sarramon; 45 above left Christian Sarramon; 45 above right Mark Ballogg, Steincamp/Designers & Architects Kevin Brown, Ken Jung, Backen, Arragonni & Ross; 45 below left Richard Glover/architects Softroom; 45 below right Ed Reeve; 46 above gettyone stone/Daniel Bosler; 46 below left Park Hyatt, Tokyo; 46 below right Katz Pictures/Jean François Pin; 47 above left Christian Sarramon; 47 above right Tim Street-Porter; 47 below Agence Top/Martin Fraudreau; 48 above left Jean Cazals; 48 above centre Michael Busselle; 48 above right Richard Glover; 48 centre © The Condé Nast Publications Ltd./*Vogue Entertaining & Travel*/Mark Burgin; 48 below Jean Cazals; 48–49 The Image Bank/G V Faint; 49 above left Hémisphères/Bertrand Rieger; 49 above right Explorer/A Evrard; 49 centre Hémisphères/Bertrand Rieger; 49 below Jason Lowe; 50–51 Michael Busselle; 52 left Gilles Rigoulet; 52 above right Christian Sarramon; 52–53 The Image Bank/Alan Becker; 53 above Christian Sarramon; 53 centre David Spero; 53 below The River Café, New York; 54 Minh & Wass; 56 Andrew Lamb/designer David Collins; 57 Conran Restaurants Ltd./David Brittain; 59 Christian Sarramon; 60 Anthony Blake Photo Library; 61 *Elle Decoration*/Matteo Manduzio; 62 Leigh Prentice; 63 Archphoto Inc./Eduard Hueber/architect Bentel + Bentel; 64 Theo van Doesburg (C.E.M. Küpper), Café Aubette, Strasbourg. Colour scheme (preceding final version) for floor and long walls of ballroom, 1927. Ink and gouache on page 21 x 14¾ in (53.3 x 37.5cm). The Museum of Modern Art, New York. Gift of Lily Auchincloss, Celeste Bartus and Marshall Cogan. Photograph © 1999 The Museum of Modern Art, New York; 64–65 Archipress/Luc Boegly; 66 above left Conran Restaurants Ltd./David Brittain; 66 above right GBH Communications/Peter Cook; 66 below Georgia Glynn-Smith; 67 Michael Moran; 68 Arcaid/Simon Kenny/Belle/designer Philippe Starck; 69 above left Richard Glover/designer Anand Zenz; 69 above right Conran Restaurants Ltd./David Brittain; 69 below left George Wright; 69 below right Paul Warchol/designed by architect Jeffrey Beers; 70 below Richard Glover/architect David Chipperfield; 70–71 Richard Glover/architect Rick Mather; 71 above right Arcaid/Nicholas Kane; 71 below left Todd Eberle/ECBPR; 71 below right Arcaid/Richard Waite; 72 above left Conran Restaurants Ltd./David Brittain; 72 above right Ed Reeve; 72 below left Hémisphères/Bertrand Gardel; 72–73 Jason Lowe; 73 above Jean Cazals; 74–75 Andreas von Einsiedel; 75 above Georgia Glynn-Smith; 75 below gettyone stone/Charles Gutpon; 76 left Taverne Agency/Mirjam Bleeker/stylist Frank Visser; 76 above right George Wright; 76 centre right Ed Reeve; 76 below right David Loftus; 77 above left Arcaid/Gisela Erlacher; 77 above right Richard Glover/architect Rick Mather; 77 centre Ray Main/Mainstream; 77 below View/Dennis Gilbert/architects Allies and Morrison; 78 above left Minh & Wass; 78 above right Andrew Lamb/designer David Collins; 78 below left Minh & Wass; 78–79 Arcaid/Nicholas Kane/Harper Mackay Architects; 79 Arcaid/Chris Gascoigne; 80 Jean Cazals; 82 Jason Lowe; 83 Agenzia Fotografica Franca Speranza/Renato Zacchia; 84 Deidi von Schaewen; 86 George Wright; 87 © The Condé Nast Publications Ltd./*Vogue Entertaining & Travel*/William Meppen; 88 Anthony Blake Picture Library/Sian Irvine; 89 © The Condé Nast Publications Ltd./*Vogue Entertaining & Travel*/George Seper; 90 Explorer/A Wolf; 91 Gruppo/Oliver Peyton/ © Jake Chessum; 93 Hémisphères/Bertrand Gardel; 94–95 Toby Glanville courtesy of Julia Fuller/Advice on Art; 96 above left Michael Busselle; 96 below left George Wright; 96–97 Jason Lowe; 97 Michael Freeman; 98 above Jean Cazals; 98 below left Christian Sarramon; 98 below right Melanie Acevedo; 99 left Jean Cazals; 99 right Melanie Acevedo; 100 Sesse Lind/courtesy of *Wallpaper**; 101 AKG London/Paul Almasy; 102 above Hémisphères/Patrick Frilet; 102 centre Axiom/Jim Holmes; 102 below gettyone stone/James Strachan; 102–103 Jeremy Hopley/Conran Octopus; 103 Jason Lowe; 104 Park Hyatt Hotel, Tokyo/John Hay; 104–105 Park Hyatt Hotel, Tokyo; 105 left © The Condé Nast Publications Ltd./*Vogue Entertaining & Travel*/Quentin Bacon; 105 above right © The Condé Nast Publications Ltd./*Vogue Entertaining & Travel*/William Meppen; 105 below right Explorer/J P Nacivet; 106 left © The Condé Nast Publications Ltd./*Vogue Entertaining & Travel*/Geoff Lung; 106 right © The Condé Nast Publications Ltd./*Vogue Entertaining & Travel*/William Meppen; 107 above left Georgia Glynn-Smith; 107 above right Geoff Lung; 107 below Jean Cazals; 108 Agence Top/A Rivière-Lecoeur; 110 Marianne Majerus; 111 Mitch Jenkins/courtesy of *Food Illustrated*; 112

above Orebro University; 112 below Ulla/Orebro University/Britt Jonsson; 114 Conran Restaurants Ltd./James Merrell; 115 PROD © DB/M Peccoux; 116 George Lang; 117 David Loftus; 118–119 Conran Restaurants Ltd./James Merrell; 120 above left © The Condé Nast Publications Ltd/*Vogue Entertaining & Travel*/Petrina Tinslay; 120 above right Conran Restaurants Ltd/David Brittain; 120 below left David Loftus; 120 below right Minh & Wass; 121 Anthony Blake Photo Library/Tim Macpherson; 122 Conran Restaurants Ltd./Georgia Glynn-Smith; 123 above left Jean Cazals; 123 above right Agence Top/Maurice Rougemont; 123 below left Agence Top/Pierre Hussenot; 123 below right Ray Main/Mainstream; 124 above Anthony Blake Photo Library/Tim Macpherson; 124 below Conran Restaurants Ltd./James Merrell; 125 *Saveur*/Maura McEvoy; 126 left JB Visual Press/H Neumann; 126 right Katz Pictures/Regina Recht; 127 left Hémisphères/Patrick Frilet; 127 right Conran Restaurants Ltd./James Merrell; 128 Conran Restaurants Ltd./Earl Carter; 129 Jean Cazals; 130 above left Hémisphères/Bertrand Gardel; 130 above right Gilles Rigoulet; 130 below left Hémisphères/Stéphane Frances; 130 below right *Marie Claire Maison*/Denis Majorel/Rozensztroch/Tiné; 131 Katz Pictures/Julian Anderson; 132–133 Alexander van Berge; 133 Gilles Rigoulet; 134 Conran Restaurants Ltd./James Merrell; 136 Ray Main/Mainstream; 137 Andreas von Einsiedel; 138 above Terence Conran; 138 below Conran Restaurants Ltd./James Merrell; 140 Minh & Wass; 141 Arcaid/Richard Waite; 142 *Saveur*; 143 The Interior Archive/Tim Goffe; 144 Agence Top/Roland Beaufre/designer Olivier Gagnière; 144–145 Georgia Glynn-Smith; 145 above right Conran Restaurants Ltd./Peter Cook; 145 below right Geoff Lung; 146 Alexander van Berge; 147 Arcaid/Nicholas Kane/Architect Mark Newson; 148 above Paul Robertson/Café Gandolfi; 148 below Geoff Lung/designer Philippe Starck; 149 above Patrick Engquist/architect Claesson Koivisto Rune Arkitektkontor; 149 below Andreas von Einsiedel; 150–151 John Gollings; 152 above left David Loftus; 152 above centre Arcaid/Niall Clutton/designer Simon Woodroffe; 152 above right Jean Cazals; 152 centre right Richard Glover; 152 below left © Wagamama/Judah Passow; 152 below right Pearce Marchbank/Studio Twenty; 153 above left Andreas von Einsiedel; 153 above centre © The Condé Nast Publications Ltd/*Vogue Entertaining & Travel*/Petrina Tinslay; 153 above right Jason Lowe; 153 centre left Patrick Engquist/architect Claesson Koivisto Rune Arkitektkontor; 153 centre Ed Reeve; 153 centre right Conran Restaurants Ltd./David Brittain; 153 below centre Belgo; 153 below right Conran Restaurants Ltd./David Brittain; 154 left Christian Sarramon; 154 right Axiom/James Morris/Wagamama; 155 above left The Ivy, London; 155 above right Big Bowl, Chicago; 155 below left Simpsons-in-the-Strand, London; 155 below right The Interior Archive/Christopher Simon Sykes; 156 above left George Wright; 156 above right *Marie Claire Maison*/Christian Sarramon/Forgeur/Marchal; 156 below left Gruppo/David Loftus; 156 below right Anthony Blake Photo Library/Tim Macpherson; 157 above Park Hyatt Hotel, Tokyo; 157 below left Paul Warchol/designer Cary Tamarkin; 157 below right Paul Warchol/designers The Rockwell Group; 158–159 Patrick McLeavey/Conran Octopus; 160 Minh & Wass; 162 Conran Restaurants Ltd./David Loftus; 163 Richard Glover/Marlin Lighting; 165 Terry Durack; 167 Debbie Patterson; 168 Magnum/Henri Cartier-Bresson; 170–171 Conran Restaurants Ltd./Jonathan Pile; 173 Hémisphères/Philippe Guignard; 174 above left Christian Sarramon; 174 above right Minh & Wass; 174 below left Gilles Rigoulet; 174 below right *Marie Claire Maison*/Tito Barberis/Bailhache/Raynaud; 175 left Jason Lowe; 175 right Katz Pictures/Giordano/Saba-Rea; 176–177 Axiom/James Morris/architects Driendl and Steixner; 176 below Jean Cazals; 177 above Ed Reeve; 177 below Axiom/James Morris/architect David Chipperfield; 178 Lars Hansson; 179 Lars Tegman; 180 left © 1999 by The New York Times Company. Reprinted by permission; 180 right Jonathan Meedes/Times Newspapers; 181 above left © The Condé Nast Publications/*Vogue Entertaining & Travel*; 181 above right *Saveur*; 181 below left The Red Guide France, courtesy of Michelin Travel Publications © 1999; 181 below right ZAGAT SURVEY; 182 above left & centre left Classic Motoring Group; 182 below left Geoff Lung; 182 right © The Condé Nast Publications Ltd./*Vogue Entertaining & Travel*/Petrina Tinslay; 183 above Andreas von Einsiedel; 183 below Anthony Blake Photo Library/Tim Macpherson; 184–185 Gilles Rigoulet; 192 Magnum/Dennis Stock.

Every effort has been made to trace the copyright holders, architects and designers and we apologize in advance for any unintentional omission and would be pleased to insert the appropriate acknowledgement in any subsequent edition.